Double Blackjack

Double Blackjack

✦

The Best and Worst Deals made by the New York Mets in their years of existence

Larry Liebenthal

iUniverse, Inc.

New York Lincoln Shanghai

Double Blackjack
The Best and Worst Deals made by the New York Mets in their years of existence

iUniverse, Inc.

For information address:
iUniverse, Inc.
2021 Pine Lake Road, Suite 100
Lincoln, NE 68512
www.iuniverse.com

ISBN: 0-595-31276-4

Printed in the United States of America

In Memoriam

For Bobby, who was the link between Willie and Barry as perennial 30-30 men.

For Tug, who made us all believers when it seemed all hope was lost.

Contents

Acknowledgements

To my family and friends, who have stood by me.

Mostly, to my "support system:" Roz and Ellen.

Foreword

Between the four professional major sports dominions in the United States and Canada, there are some 112 franchises in operation, as of this writing. Inventorying the leagues alphabetically in order (and possibly in order of preference to some people), Major League Baseball, the National Basketball Association, the National Football League, and the National Hockey League have toeholds in 47 different regions. "Hair-splitters" might argue that Milwaukee and Green Bay are separate entities, and many fans in the New York Metropolitan area would certainly disagree about including New Jersey as part of their "neighborhood." New Jersey fans could have the same justifiable "beef."

There was once a famous advertising slogan for a now-defunct bank that said, "Flushing ain't Flatbush!" What the advertisers were trying to convey was that their client could suit the needs of their depositors, no matter where they lived. However, this particular phrase still strikes a chord in the hearts of New York baseball fans, whether or not they were able to remember the years the Dodgers played at Ebbets Field and the Giants were at the PoloGrounds or the heart wrenching time when they suddenly deserted the city, or how their "foster child" came to be adopted by the "Fun City" forlorn faithful.

This text is dedicated to them, the New York Mets' fans of the past 42 years (hence the title *Double Blackjack*) present, and future; former fans, fair-weather fans, or truly dedicated fans who can quote every statistic and every personal detail of every Met from Don Aase to Don Zimmer. You're the ones that kept the franchise going even when it had seemingly given up on improving itself and attracting a new audience. You're the ones they hand out the cheap plastic gifts to on Fan Appreciation Day; you're the ones who keep coming back for more punishment when many others would have "run the white flag up the pole." While not nearly quite so melodramatic (or destitute or desperate), Mets fans are similar to the "Okies" in John Steinbeck's classic *The Grapes of Wrath*. As Ma Joad stubbornly averred, "they can't keep the people down forever, and *we're* the people!" That's in a small measure akin to rooting for the Mets, or as one writer quipped, "To err is human, to forgive is to be a Met fan."

Introduction

I was born in the Bronx in November 1960, approximately a half-year before the Mets technically commenced (as Casey Stengel was fond of saying) as a franchise in New York. After living in Parkchester for eight years, my family relocated to Flushing, Queens. Thus, you can see right off the bat (no pun intended) that my loyalties as a Big Apple professional baseball fan have been divided since before my adolescence.

The Dodgers and Giants fled what they ostensibly considered the respective urban blight of Flatbush and upper Manhattan for the sunnier (and in some instances, windier and shakier) climate of California after the 1957 season. One thing the former fanatics of each team, who shared perhaps the most intense rivalry in American sports history, had in common was their vehement hatred of the clubs' owners, especially the cold-hearted opportunistic Walter O'Malley. O'Malley had the team's 3,000-mile southwest egress planned long in advance. Four years earlier, he had swapped Triple-A minor league affiliates with Philip Wrigley, owner of the Chicago Cubs, and thus got his foothold in Los Angeles. In fact, the bandbox stadium the Los Angeles Angels used to play their home games in from 1961–64 was called Wrigley Park, and was originally owned by the Cubs, and then the Dodgers (although they never actually "bled Dodger blue" there).

So, it was just a matter of getting the approval of the other seven National League teams to approve the move—O'Malley also coyly knew he needed a "co-conspirator" to legitimize the transaction. If, as the saying goes, "politics makes strange bedfellows," then O'Malley found himself perhaps the strangest ally: Giants' owner Horace Stoneham. While O'Malley was at least outwardly very callous about the transfer, Stoneham had tried to act like the victim, saying he truly wanted to stay, but waning attendance and the Bay Area prospects had made any another choice impossible. Supposedly, a deal had surreptitiously been in the making involving power broker Robert Moses, who was New York Commissioner of Public Works, and Mayor Robert Wagner.

Moses, who had been the driving force behind the building of many of New York City's great transportation and commerce facilities (including major highways, bridges, tunnels, parks, beaches, World's Fairs, airports, and many others) was allegedly trying to get both teams to stay by offering to build new ballparks, partially at taxpayers' expense.

However, the city could have literally given O'Malley the key to Central Park, and he was still adamant about "going Hollywood." The National League board of governors meekly agreed and in one fell swoop (just 4 years after the Giants won the World Series, and only 3 years after the Brooklyn faithful finally were not required to say "Wait 'til next year!") New York National League fans lost both their teams. This left the New York Yankees to "run the table" alone, but, as one writer once said, "Rooting for the Yankees is like rooting for U.S. Steel or General Motors." Although the Yanks won 3 pennants and 2 World Championships between 1958–1961 (including the "M&M" boys chasing "the Babe"), a huge unfilled void existed in the "Fun City" baseball domain.

So, the foundation was laid for the formation of a new New York baseball franchise but, even back when things were far simpler in the late '50's, teams didn't just come "out of thin air." However, in a literal sense, it may have been foul air, specifically cigar smoke that began the Mets' evolution. O'Malley was a renowned "stogie-toker," as was a gentleman who, at one time, may have been the most powerful person in baseball but was subsequently undermined by O'Malley: Branch Rickey. To that date, two of Rickey's greatest innovations as a general manager were the development of the farm system with the St. Louis Cardinals in the 1930's, and his initiating the breaking of the color barrier while GM and majority owner of the Brooklyn Dodgers in the late 1940's. However, part of O'Malley's maneuvering to control the Dodgers (and to ultimately take flight with them) was to clandestinely buy up all minority club shares and then coax Rickey into relinquishing enough shares for O'Malley to have more than 50% ownership. Rickey had waited for a long time to get even and, in some measure, he did.

When no other major league franchises offered to relocate to New York (possibly intimidated by the Yankees' presence) and in another effort to "buck the system," Rickey announced in July 1959 the creation of a third major league, known as the Continental League. It was tentatively scheduled to begin operations as early as the following season and was planning to have franchises (in alphabetical order) within the cities of Atlanta, Buffalo, Denver, Houston, Minneapolis-St. Paul, Montreal, New York, and Toronto. To prove what a visionary Rickey was, today 7 of these 8 metropolises have existing major league teams, and Buffalo, which has a thriving minor league affiliate, barely missed out on the bidding for a new area of competition prior to the 1992 Expansion Draft.

At the time, though, few people (especially O'Malley and the other powers that ruled Major League Baseball) were calling Rickey a visionary; among many epithets, the kindest was "Bolshevik." This was a direct challenge to MLB's unique anti-trust exemption, which it had enjoyed with the U.S. Supreme Court's grudging blessing since 1922. As a compromise, MLB agreed to expand for the first time since the short-lived Federal League in 1914, and four new teams were allowed to join their exalted ranks. Two franchises, the Los Angeles Angels and the new Washington Senators (which came about when the Griffith family abandoned the nation's capital for the "untamed" frontier of Minnesota and renamed their club the Twins), were initiated into the American League in 1961. One year later, the Houston Colt .45's became one of the two new N.L. entries. Along with them, fulfilling a dream many baseball fans in the N.Y. Tri-State area had all but given up on, came the New York Metropolitans.

The two extra squads in each circuit meant that the 154-game schedule, which for so long had neatly fit eight teams (22 games against all other teams in your league: 11 at home and 11 on the road), now had to be expanded to 162. This was still long before regional divisional play was implemented, which meant that both expansion teams in each league had to face the toughest competition *18* times. This was especially rough on the Metropolitans (or Mets as they would become popularly known), since four different established teams had won the pennant in the last four years, and a fifth, the San Francisco Giants, would accomplish the feat this year after a grueling three-game playoff with the Los Angeles Dodgers. In fact, the league was so top-heavy in the first N.L. expansion season that every incumbent team, except the Milwaukee Braves, increased their 1961 victory total and a record 4 teams won 90 or more games.

Mets' fans should have "seen the handwriting on the wall" very early on in the season. While the Pittsburgh Pirates "burst out of the starting blocks" and won their first 10 games, the New York Mets were "spinning their wheels" and lost their first 9! In other words, they were actually behind more games in the standings (9½) than they had participated in. Another bad harbinger occurred when, on their first road trip, several Mets players got stuck in a St. Louis hotel elevator for two hours. The Mets' fortunes did not get any better *on* the field, as they finished 40-120, eighteen games behind the 9th place Chicago Cubs. They also came in last in batting average (.240), doubles (166), fielding percentage (.967), pitching strikeouts (772), runs allowed (948), shutouts (4), saves (10), and earned run average (5.04). However, they *did* manage to *lead* in one team category: errors committed (210). There were encouraging signs, though. Their centerfielder, former Philadelphia Phillie Richie Ashburn, was not only their hitting leader with a .306 average, but he finished third in the league in walks with 81. Their best power hitter, ex-Milwaukee Brave first baseman/outfielder Frank Thomas, came in sixth in the home run race with 34, and even added 94 RBI.

Truthfully, Mets' fans couldn't have cared less about team or individual stats, and the club could have virtually lost *every* game that season, as far as *they* were concerned. They were just happy to have a National League home team to root for. However, the "honeymoon" could not last forever; the Mets' management knew it would have to build a strong organization and field a contender, and within a reasonable amount of time. New York fans are reputed for being the most appreciative and the most knowledgeable, and the Mets' front office knew it could not "pull the wool over their eyes."

Thus, this is the basis for this literary undertaking, to examine the 21 best and 21 worst personnel decisions ever made by Mets' management. These had to be limited to front office maneuvers: to start second-guessing any on-the-field judgments would have required a novel longer than *War and Peace, Dr. Zhivago,* and *Nicholas Nickleby* combined. I've tried to arrange the stories in both parameters of importance and in "chronological order by date," to quote a "Yogi-ism." As a writer and a fan, I hope this makes for enjoyable reading.

#1 High Quality Move—A 'Terrific' Way to Start

At the suggestion of young pitching prospect Dick Selma, a former teammate of George "Tom" Seaver at USC, General Manager George Weiss decides to match Seaver's contract offer from Atlanta in 1966. The Braves had violated NCAA rules by signing Seaver after his senior varsity baseball season had already begun.

Major League Baseball Commissioner William "Spike" Eckert voided Seaver's contract and the Mets, Dodgers, and Braves (sequenced in that order due to the Mets' poorer record than the Dodgers and the Braves' blunder) were given the chance to pick Seaver's name out of a hat to be allowed to rightfully sign him. As Branch Rickey was fond of saying, "Luck is the residue of design," and the Mets were fortunate enough to be able to obtain the rights to Seaver's services.

Spending only one year in the minors, Seaver was promoted to the parent club, won 16 games for a last-place team and earned National League Rookie-of-the-Year honors. As a Met, he had four different 20-victory seasons (and narrowly missed out in two others), accomplished an all-time record of nine consecutive seasons with 200 or more strikeouts (leading the N.L. 5 times), won the N.L. ERA title three times, pitched five one-hit games (carrying no-hitters into the 9th inning thrice) and, on Earth Day 1970 at Shea Stadium, struck out 19 San Diego Padres (still co-holding the team record), and astonishingly fanned the last 10 batters (another all-time MLB mark). After receiving the N.L. Cy Young Award 3 times in a 7-season period (and having one elude him in 1971 when he himself felt he had his best overall pitching performance), and being a key member of two pennants and a World Championship, Seaver was quite justifiably known as "Tom Terrific" and also considered "The Franchise."

In 1992, Seaver became the first player enshrined in the Baseball Hall-of-Fame as a New York Met. He is also the only member in the organization's history to have his uniform number (41) retired by the team as a player, the other two being legendary Met managers Casey Stengel and Gil Hodges.

#1 Low Quality Move—The Erection of "Grant's Tomb"

As the structure of the baseball world was changing in the mid-1970's, the Mets' management stubbornly refused to "bend with the breeze." This was partially due to the death of Mrs. Joan W. Payson in 1975, who had been the Mets' principal owner since they were an expansion team in 1962. As a result, Chairman of the Board M. Donald Grant usurped the main decision-making power of the organization.

So, as the negotiating position of major league players strengthened (through the advent of a Collective Bargaining Agreement, arbitration, and eventually free agency), Grant sought to dismantle the nucleus of the teams that had been so successful during the late 1960's and early 1970's (having only one losing season and no last-place finishes between 1969–1976). At different intervals, when it suited him, whether or not he got anything other than cash in return, he began trading off long-time stalwarts such as Tug McGraw, Rusty Staub, Bud Harrelson, Wayne Garrett, Jerry Grote, John Milner, Jon Matlack, Duffy Dyer, Jerry Koosman and Ken Boswell, just to name a few.

However, the ultimate outrage came on June 15, 1977, when rather than agree to a guaranteed long-term deal with Tom Seaver, Grant traded him to the Cincinnati Reds and did not get any front-line talent in return. This is not to cast aspersions on the character or abilities of Steve Henderson, Doug Flynn, Pat Zachry or Dan Norman, the players received in exchange for Seaver. It simply, at the risk of sounding exaggerated, signaled a death knell for the Mets organization and started a tailspin from which they would not fully emerge for seven years.

Perhaps the roots of Grant's deep resentment started at a 1973 mid-season team meeting when he addressed the team in the clubhouse, superficially as a pep-talk, to reassure them that the club was not going be broken up and that injuries to many vital players had played a major role in the Mets' poor performance. In the middle of this "heart warming" speech, "flaky" southpaw ace reliever Frank "Tug" McGraw screamed out, "Ya gotta believe!" He always claimed he was just underscoring Grant's sentiments; but Grant took it as a personal insult, felt embarrassed and satirized, stormed out of the clubhouse, and never forgave McGraw. McGraw apologized in four different venues: privately, in front of the team, in public through the media, and in his autobiography, *Screwball.* That phrase, "Ya gotta believe!," by the way, became the Mets' rallying cry of their incredible comeback, in what is referred to as the "Minor Miracle of '73."

Led by McGraw, who had straightened himself out after a horrendous 0-6 start, the Mets won 21 of their last 29 games, finishing the season just three games over .500, but that was enough to clinch the N.L. Eastern Division, since no one else from their "expedition" had a winning record. In the NLCS, they then faced the heavily favored Cincinnati Reds, who'd led all of baseball with 99 victories, and who featured eventual Hall-of-Famers Johnny Bench, Joe Morgan, and Tony Perez on their squad. They also had a feisty "jack-of-all-trades" whose position this year happened to be leftfield and whose 3rd career batting title enabled him to win the M.V.P. Award: Pete Rose. Nevertheless, the Mets refused to be intimidated, held the Reds to just 8 runs in the five games (5 of them coming on solo homers), and even became involved in a donnybrook after Harrelson refused to back down to Rose's venting his frustrations. The Mets won the pennant and extended the defending champion Oakland A's to 7 games in the World Series, despite a key injury to Daniel "Rusty" Staub, who'd separated his right shoulder while making an incredible catch in NLCS Game 4. In fact, playing without the full use of his right arm, Staub led all participants in hits (11), average (.423) and tied for the lead in RBI with 6. He could easily have been selected Series M.V.P. even in a losing effort.

Things went badly for the Mets in 1974, especially for McGraw, who wound up relinquishing his closer role due to an excess of blown saves. This was all the impetus Grant needed to get rid of whom he considered his main antagonist. Grant, for whatever motives, chose to hold a grudge; it must be something about the name, similar to the way Ulysses S. Grant, who had lost many comrades and subordinates to the Confederate Army during the Civil War, never forgave the Southern States, even after they were readmitted to the Union. Perhaps *M.D.* Grant shared a kinship with his authoritative predecessor with the same surname, *U.S.* Grant.

McGraw was traded to Philadelphia during the off-season, but Mets fans at least had time to "digest" that trade. The Seaver trade has left a sour taste to this day.

#2 High Quality Move—The Prodigal Son Returns

It had taken 5 years, 6 months, and a day (but who's counting?) to correct the injustice done to loyal Mets' fans, but on December 16, 1982, Tom Seaver was reacquired from where he was so unceremoniously dealt to, the Cincinnati Reds. By now, the Mets were under new ownership (Nelson Doubleday & Fred Wilpon) and, while they were trying to rebuild the organization virtually from scratch, they made possibly the best public relations maneuver of their careers. Ironically, Seaver had been part of a similar morass that accelerated his original expulsion from the Big Apple: a major league front office hell-bent on holding the line against increasing player salaries, namely General Manager Dick Wagner of Cincinnati.

Seaver's "re-debut" as a Met on Opening Day at Shea Stadium on April 5, 1983 is considered one of the greatest and most emotional days in Mets' history. Seaver pitched 6 shutout innings against the Philadelphia Phillies, opposing 4-time N.L. Cy Young Award winner Steve Carlton, who had also been involved years ago in a controversial trade from his original club, the St. Louis Cardinals. Although Seaver did not get a decision, the Mets nonetheless went on to win 2-0, sending the fans home ecstatic and hopeful for the team's chances.

Unfortunately, the excitement quickly wore off, as the Mets wound up finishing last in the N.L. Eastern Division for the second straight time and for the 5th time in the previous 7 years. However, the fans and front office alike were emboldened by the expeditious development of homegrown talent such as Mookie Wilson, Hubie Brooks, Wally Backman, and Darryl Strawberry. A much-valued addition to the team occurred (coincidentally on the June 15th trading deadline) when the Mets obtained All-Star first baseman Keith Hernandez, who'd already won a batting title and an M.V.P., from St. Louis. At the time, Hernandez bore the label of "damaged goods" because of his past.

As for the so-called publicity stunt, Seaver pitched as well as a 38-year-old, 17-year veteran can be expected to perform for a cellar-dweller. He finished 9-13, with 5 complete games (including 2 shutouts), didn't miss any of his 34 scheduled starts, amassed a 3.55 ERA and had 86 walks and 135 strikeouts in 231 innings. The future finally looked bright again for the Mets and their faithful.

#2 Low Quality Move—The Franchise "Re-vanishes"

There's an old adage that "no good deed ever goes unpunished." Just when the Mets looked like they were rising from their ashes, with their most popular player in the midst of their renaissance, history chillingly repeated itself and "The Franchise" was suddenly gone again.

As part of the settlement of the 1981 Baseball strike, every team was required to leave several players exposed in a "compensation pool" for when veteran free agents are signed. Tom Seaver was one of the players not protected by the Mets, considered a good gamble at the time that no team would select him and thus be obligated to honor his contract. However, when relief pitcher Dennis Lamp played out his option with the Chicago White Sox and was subsequently signed by the Toronto Blue Jays, Seaver was quickly "snatched out of the pool" and became a member of "The *Pale* Hose."

Tom won 31 games over the next two seasons, including his 300th career victory which happened to transpire in the city in which he earned his greatest fame, New York; except that it took place at *Yankee* Stadium on August 4, 1985 and actually upstaged the pregame ceremonies retiring "Bronx Bomber" legend Phil "Scooter" Rizzuto's number.

The snafu was blamed on incoming Mets' skipper Davy Johnson, who supposedly didn't want to be himself upstaged by Seaver, and who wanted to build a young pitching staff literally from the ground up. Johnson, to this day, staunchly denies this and strongly avers that this was strictly a personnel move made by the front office, possibly monetarily motivated. Whatever the case may be, Seaver was not allowed to be part of the Mets' resurgence of the mid-1980's and could probably have been of assistance to them in both 1984 and 1985 when they challenged for the division title but came up short both times. In another twist of irony, Seaver was sitting in the opposing dugout when the Mets finally made it "over the hump" and got to the World Series. He had won seven games for the Boston Red Sox in 1986 before being placed on the disabled list, but was nevertheless on hand when "The *Crimson* Hose" pulled off their own miracle pennant in the ALCS, coming back from the brink of elimination vs. the California Angels. Seaver could only watch helplessly as the New York Mets, the team he had become inexorably associated with, turned the tables and won their second World Championship.

#3 High Quality Move—The "Ol' Perfesser" Emeritus

At a press conference in May 1961, the National League office announced it would be replenishing New York with a new baseball franchise as well as placing an expansion team in Houston. Former New York Yankees' manager Charles "Casey" Stengel had just been fired the previous October after his team had been upset in the World Series by the Pittsburgh Pirates. His response at the time was that he'd "never make the mistake of being 70 [years old] again." Now, still two months shy of his 71st birthday, he is chosen for the managerial post of the New York Metropolitans, who are scheduled to begin operations the following season. This time, Stengel quips that it's an honor to be able to manage the New York *Knickerbockers*, who are actually a local professional *basketball* team.

Thus began the tenure of one the most beloved figures in Mets' history, as skipper during their formative and, consequently, least triumphant years. In fact, the Mets would set a dubious mark of having the worst single season record of the 20th Century, going 40-120 in 1962 for a .250 winning percentage, finishing 80 games under .500 and 60½ games out of first place. However, because Stengel was such a popular figure in the Big Apple (dating back to his days as a player with the Brooklyn Dodgers during the 1910's and with the New York Giants during the 1920's) and was able to manipulate the media so deftly, he helped soften the blow of the constant losing.

Additionally, New York N.L. baseball fans were starved for *any* kind of team to root for since they had been abandoned four years earlier when the Dodgers and Giants relocated to California.

"The Ol' Perfesser" would accrue an aggregate 175-404 win-loss record in 3 ½ seasons as Mets' manager (compared with 1,751 victories and 1,463 defeats he had compiled in his previous 21 years) before being forced to permanently "hang up his spikes" after suffering a broken hip. He stayed on in a consultant role, became the first Met to have his uniform number (37) retired, and was finally inducted into the Baseball Hall-of-Fame in 1966. Casey, by chance, died within the same week as Mrs. Payson. Their demises, which happened so closely together in terms of occurrence, perhaps portended bad tidings for the entire New York Mets organization.

#3 Low Quality Move—The Captain Mans The Wheel

New York City, being the media capital of the American sports world, has never been a utopia for a major league baseball manager. No matter how popular or successful they are, especially with the increased exposure due to television, all Mets' managers (and Yankees' managers, for that matter) have come under constant scrutiny. Some learn how to deal with it and others don't or simply won't.

Casey Stengel, Gil Hodges, Lawrence "Yogi" Berra, Davy Johnson, and Bobby Valentine were arguably the best managers, both in terms of public relations and on-the-field success in Mets' history. However, the organization has also made some poor choices to guide the helm. "Cobra" Joe Frazier, George Bamberger, Derrel "Bud" Harrelson, Dallas Green, and, currently, Art Howe spring to mind as skippers who were or are ill-fitted to "running the Mets' ship." Others, such as Wes Westrum and Joe Torre (both coincidentally catchers during their playing days), exhibited admirable managerial skills (always stressing fundamental-soundness to both youngsters and veterans, being well-organized, and good handlers of players) while with the Mets, but did not possess the necessary available personnel to field consistently contending squads.

But, by far the worst choice the Mets' organization ever handed the major league reins to was Jeff Torborg. He had just come off a successful run with the Chicago White Sox and the Mets decided not to replace Bud Harrelson after the 1991 season with an in-house minor league manager (such as Mike Cubbage); they opted instead for Torborg. His 1½ seasons were marred by numerous confrontations with prima donnas such as Vince Coleman and Bobby Bonilla, several sex scandals (involving Coleman, Dwight Gooden, Daryl Boston, and David Cone) and the infamous "bleaching" incident perpetrated by Bret Saberhagen on unsuspecting sportswriters. Torborg's tumultuous tenure was mercifully terminated two months into the 1993 season, in which the Mets finished dead last for the first time in a decade and is considered by most observers as their most miserable overall season to date.

As for Torborg, he has been able to gain managerial employment for other major league franchises, but the one entry on his résumé he would like to permanently expunge is his term with New York's National League franchise.

#4 High Quality Move—"This is the Stuff Dreams are Made of"

Modern professional baseball players have much more leverage than their predecessors of as recently as three decades ago. Now, players can take salary disputes and disciplinary cases to arbitration, demand trades or refuse assignments, renegotiate long-term contracts at will, and literally get away with criminal charges up to and including *murder*. Before the Major League Baseball Players Association developed any real "teeth," players had virtually no recourse. They could hold out to try to get more money from their club or retire if they didn't want to be traded.

That's precisely what Donn Clendenon threatened to do in the winter of 1969. At 33 years old, he had spent 7 productive full seasons as a first baseman with the Pittsburgh Pirates. Playing half his games in the capacious "non-confines" of Forbes Field and during the most pitching-dominated decade in almost 50 years, Clendenon was still able to average 15 home runs and 70 RBI a season, while batting .280 over that span. However, it was his free-swinging approach that made him a favorite with Buc fans, accumulating 840 lifetime whiffs, including a then-record 163 strikeouts in 1968.

Strictly as a strategy to preserve their young prospects, Clendenon was left unprotected by the Pirates in the 1969 Expansion Draft and was one of the first players selected by the Montreal Expos. Hardly had Donn gotten a chance to obtain his passport when he was traded to the Houston Astros, a month before the beginning of spring training. Clendenon is an intelligent, well-educated, sensitive black man, much of the same character as the late Curt Flood, who as fate would have it, initiated a similar quixotic fight against baseball's "reserve clause" before the end of the calendar year. Donn had experienced enough bigotry growing up in Missouri, playing in Southern cities where intolerance was the norm, and wanted no part of "The Lone Star State."

He refused to report to the Astros and submitted his voluntary retirement request to the National League. Not wanting to cause more turbulence in an already stormy era, and in an effort to prevent further tarnishing of Major League

Baseball's image by forcing a popular player into retirement, both new Commissioner Bowie Kuhn and Expos' owner Charles Bronfman intervene and negate the deal.

Clendenon reports to Montreal, but is still far from being a "happy camper." He is again reputedly making serious overtures about quitting baseball if he is not sent to a more promising franchise than the dreadful fledgling Expos. On June 15th (there's that date, again), Donn gets his wish as the New York Mets, who are solidly in 2nd place in the N.L. Eastern Division (and just coming off a team record 11-game winning streak), acquire him for four minor leaguers. Clendenon fits in immediately as the right-handed "initial sacker" platoon, complementing original Met Ed Kranepool. Collectively, they finish the 1969 regular season with a composite first baseman offensive productivity of 27 homers and 100 RBI! Clendenon exhibited power, presence, and leadership in his 72 contests with the Mets that year and it translated in the standings: New York came from a 5-game deficit behind the Chicago Cubs before Clendenon was on their roster to an 8-game runaway lead at season's end.

Incredibly, Clendenon sits on the bench the entire NLCS, as the Atlanta Braves' southpaws account for only 2 of the team's 26 innings pitched in the three-game Met sweep. Perhaps it was this snub that inspired Clendenon to make the Baltimore Orioles pay with a vengeance. He started four of the five games, slammed three critical home runs, drove in 4, scored 4, and amassed 15 total bases in 14 at bats for a five-game World Series record slugging percentage of 1.071. He also made several outstanding defensive plays, snuffing potential Baltimore rallies, and helped manager Gil Hodges argue the famous "trial by shoe polish," in the 6th inning of the clincher. It was Clendenon who first attested that Cleon Jones hit been hit on the shoe with a pitched ball, but home plate umpire Lou DiMuro was originally not "buying it." Hodges then produced the polish-stained ball and Jones was given first base on an "HBP." Then, Clendenon followed with his third round-tripper of the Series and the rest is history. Perhaps Donn's ways of expressing his difference of opinion were a precursor to his future profession as an attorney-at-law in Ohio (he also owned a restaurant in Atlanta while still an active player). These could be viable reasons why Donn felt he didn't absolutely need baseball.

Clendenon was chosen the Series' Most Valuable Player: not bad for a man ready to "hang 'em up" for good as lately as four months ago.

#4 Low Quality Move—Patience with Oysters Yields Pearls

When the New York Mets and Houston Astros first joined the National League in 1962, they were given a very thin choice of potential with which to build from. The ten American League teams did not have to participate in the Expansion Draft and the incumbent N.L. franchises were required to offer only 15 players in their entire organizations and could take one back off the "exposure list" every time somebody got picked. The Astros, who went after much younger talent than the Mets did, finished ahead of them in the standings the first six years they were both in existence.

Occasionally, the Mets were able to catch "lightning in a bottle," such as when they signed former Grambling football star Cleon Jones. They "home grew" several other position players, slowly developed a proficient youthful pitching staff (including Tom Seaver, Jerry Koosman, Gary Gentry, Nolan Ryan, Jim McAndrew, Tug McGraw, et al.) and pulled off a few shrewd trades for valuable veterans like Jerry Grote, Tommie Agee, Dr. Ron Taylor, Ed "The Glider" Charles, Art Shamsky, Don Cardwell, Al Weis and, perhaps the last piece of the puzzle, Donn Clendenon.

By the time 1969 and the next wave of expansion rolled around (thus necessitating splitting both the A.L. & N.L. into two divisions), the Mets and Astros were headed in opposite directions. Houston lost heavily in the '69 Expansion Draft, which flip-flopped from its '62 counterpart. Now, *no* existing teams were exempt and they could only protect their *top* 15 prospects, with otherwise the previous format intact. The Mets, however, emerged relatively unscathed, had 27 more victories than in 1968 and won the World Series. Houston, additionally, was placed in the same division as the team that wound up dominating the N.L. for the next decade: the Cincinnati Reds.

Between 1970–1979, "The Big Red Machine" would win 6 division titles, 4 pennants and 2 World Championships. Three of the four times Cincy didn't head the N.L. West pack, the Los Angeles Dodgers won the division and the pennant. The Astros, meanwhile, were beset by strange happenings on and off the field. Donald Wilson's committing suicide and Cesar Cedeño's killing his girl-friend (and being able to plea-bargain his way out of it) are just two of the more bizarre incidents.

Thus, it only seemed natural for their loyal, knowledgeable followers to expect that the Mets were poised to dominate in the N.L. East for several years. They were, after all, in a weaker division (with perennial losers such as the Pirates, the Cubs, and the Phillies) and were in possession of a fairly young, cohesive and capable team. Unfortunately, numerous bad trades of their own prospects proved to be their undoing. Of all the position players they got rid of and received almost nothing in return for, Amos Otis is always one of the first that springs to mind.

Going into the 1968 season, the Mets publicity department had been touting that they'd soon have an all-Alabama outfield: Jones, Agee, and Otis. While Jones did his consistently fine work, both Agee and Otis faltered. At least Agee had a legitimate excuse: he had been beaned by St. Louis Cardinals' pitcher Bob Gibson during spring training and didn't fully recover for over a year. Otis, however, simply fell victim to what many observers would term as the "small-town hick who couldn't handle the pressures of playing in the big city" syndrome. Otis did well at every Met minor league affiliate, but struggled badly when given the chance at the major league level. So, just 6½ weeks after the Mets celebrated their improbable championship with a ticker-tape parade, Otis was shipped to the Kansas City Royals for third baseman Joe Foy.

While Foy bombed miserably, Otis went on to fashion an incredible career with the Royals. In his 14 seasons in K.C., he collected nearly 2,000 hits, includ-ing 365 doubles and 193 homers, close to 1,000 RBI and over 300 stolen bases. He also led the Royals to 4 A.L. West titles and 1 pennant. In the 1980 World Series, he batted .478 with 3 homers and 7 RBI, although the Royals lost to the Philadelphia Phillies in six games.

The Mets' faithful can only ponder if Otis could have been able to produce so prodigiously for them if only given a fair chance. The last sources they can seek sympathy from are Astros' fans.

#5 High Quality Move—"The Quiet Man"

Baseball fans were played a cruel joke on All Fools Day 1972, when the MLBPA called the first general strike in the history of American professional sports. There were numerous issues involved, including arbitration, players' rights to refuse trades under the "10-and-5" pact, owners' contributions to the pension plan, etc.

However, this was nothing compared to the horrid events of the next day, when Mets' manager Gil Hodges suffered a massive fatal heart attack, just two days before his 48th birthday. This was a terrible shock not only to the baseball world, but also to many people who had admired Hodges throughout his career as a ballplayer and manager. He had been known as "The Quiet Man" all through his 10 full seasons with the Brooklyn Dodgers, during the period they were referred to as "The Boys of Summer." Hodges had originally signed with the Dodgers as a catcher in 1942, played two seasons in the minors and actually got a "cup of coffee" with "The Brooks" at the end of 1943. It was really more like a "quick sip," as he saw action in only one game, playing third base, striking out in his two official times at bat, but drawing a walk and stealing a base in his other plate appearance. Had the circumstances of the era been different, Hodges might have stuck with the club the following season.

"Uncle Sam" had different plans for Mr. Hodges as for the next two years, he was a Marine Leatherneck in combat, not a Brooklyn Dodger on a ball field. After his honorable discharge with a distinguished service record, it was back to the minors for some more seasoning with the Dodgers' Triple-A affiliate, the Montreal Royals. Gil was promoted to the majors as a back-up catcher to Bruce Edwards in 1947, appearing in 28 games (24 of them behind the plate), but batted only .156 with just 1 home run in 77 at bats. He also made one pinch-hitting appearance in the Subway Series vs. the New York Yankees, while Edwards caught every inning of all seven games, after which Brooklyn was again left repeating their hackneyed adage, "Wait 'til next year!"

In 1948, the Dodgers added former Negro Leagues' star catcher Roy Campanella to their arsenal and he soon displaced Edwards as the number-one backstop. Gil seemed to be ready to be relegated to third-string catcher, a possible utility player and part-time pinch-hitter, when owner/GM Branch Rickey traded popular veteran second baseman Eddie Stanky to the Boston Braves. This created a ripple effect in the organization: Jackie Robinson, who had broken MLB's color barrier the year before, was able to return to his more natural position at the "keystone;" Hodges wound up appearing in 134 contests, 96 as the regular first baseman and 38 more as a catcher. Then, in 1949, the Dodgers were able to add their third black man to the roster in as many years, pitcher Don Newcombe, who would finish 17-8 (being part of a four-way tie for the N.L. lead in shutouts with five) and win N.L. Rookie-of-the-Year. More importantly, the productivity of their "youngsters," combined with their established nucleus of Harold "Peewee" Reese, Billy Cox, Carl "The Reading Rifle" Furillo, Elwin "Preacher" Roe, Joe Hatten, and Ralph Branca, helped the Dodgers win the pennant and again faced the Yankees in the Series. A true rookie in his own right, centerfielder Edwin "Duke" Snider, would eventually team with Gil to give the Dodgers as formidable a righty-lefty power tandem as there's ever been. Unfortunately, they both stumbled badly in the Series (hitting a combined .184), which directly led to their team getting beaten in five games.

This slump was nothing compared to the one Hodges experienced three years later, once again in the World Series vs. the dreaded Yankees. He'd had a remarkable regular season: he was second in the league in homers (32), fourth in RBI (104), second in walks (107), tied for fourth in slugging percentage (.500), third in home run percentage [the number of homers per 100 at bats] (6.3) while playing every inning of every Dodgers game, even leading all first basemen in assists. Gil's teammates had voted him the team's M.V.P. and after losing the pennant in the last inning of their last game each of the two previous seasons, Hodges & Co. seemed loaded for bear to finally win that elusive Championship. The only trouble was that Gil seemed to have shut down his offensive production as soon as the post-season started. He went into perhaps the most horrendous drought at the most inopportune time any baseball fan has ever witnessed. Hodges literally went "oh-fer" the '52 Series, not collecting a single hit in 21 times at bat, as the Dodgers again went down to defeat, this time in the full seven games.

Nearly any other player would have been literally "booed out of town," or at least forever been "branded with the goat horns." Knowledgeable Dodgers' fans knew better than to simply blame Gil for the Series loss, and instead, stood more firmly behind him than ever. In fact, before the 7th game, many residents of the Kings County borough bestowed a spontaneous collective prayer upon Hodges. Many Catholic churches (to which denomination he was a member of) throughout Brooklyn had vigils and candle-lighting ceremonies the morning of October 7 in the hopes of summoning some divine providence to help Hodges and thus benefit his team.

Perhaps their prayers were finally answered (although in delayed fashion) nearly three years to the day later when the Dodgers finally shook off the spell the Yankees seemed to have them under and finally captured a World Championship. This Series, too, went the distance, but this time "The Boys of Summer" prevailed and Hodges himself received a certain amount of retribution: he drove in both runs in the Dodgers' 2-0 clinching victory at Yankee Stadium on October 4, 1955.

Many baseball fans will argue that the Dodgers faithful may have inadvertently made a deal with the devil by praying so hard for a title; many Dodger fans are still convinced that owner Walter O'Malley actually *was* the devil! Less than two years later, the Dodgers, along with their archrivals, the New York Giants, were on their way out of The Big Apple and headed for the Golden State. The loyalty of their fans (and the revenue they had produced so that the greedy ownerships could "carpetbag" when it suited them) meant nothing either to O'Malley or Giants' owner Horace Stoneham.

In his full decade (plus fragments of two other seasons) as a Brooklyn Dodger, Gil Hodges played 1,531 games, had 5,581 at bats, rapped out 1,784 hits (for a .320 batting average), smacked 298 home runs, and amassed 1,049 RBI and 765 bases-on-balls. He enjoyed two more productive years in Los Angeles (even contributing to their 1959 Championship with a .391 average in the Series) before his knees began troubling him and reducing him to a part-time player. Statistics, though, don't tell anywhere near the whole story of what Gil Hodges meant to baseball. His quiet leadership, steadying influence, consistent productivity, and his stature as a pillar of the community say as much about the man as any box score ever did. The fact that as of this writing he is still not enshrined in Baseball's Hall-of-Fame is a further stain on MLB's reputation.

Very much like a soap opera, the story does not end there. Hodges was selected by the Mets in the '62 Expansion Draft, but was only able to participate in 65 games over 2 years and hit just 9 homers with 20 RBI. The Mets then gave him his unconditional release so he could take the job as manager of another expansion team, the reincarnation of the Washington Senators. Given limited talent to work with (a familiar theme in Met lore), Hodges nonetheless improved the Senators' record gradually in each of his five seasons at their helm, while honing his own "skippering" skills. After the 1967 season, he was offered the position of Mets' manager, but Nats' owner Bob Short refused to release Hodges from his contract unless the Mets sent back a player in return as compensation. Unhesitatingly, Mets GM "Fireman" Johnny Murphy sent rookie pitcher Bill Denehy (who was 1-7 with a 4.70 ERA) to Washington, and "The Quiet Man" was on his way to make some noise in New York.

Incorporating a platoon system popularized by his former mentor Casey Stengel, Hodges helped make losing, which the Mets had formerly taken in stride, unpalatable.

Then, in 1969, it all came together and the Miracle Mets became as endearing to the fans of New York as their Brooklyn Dodger counterparts had been almost a decade-and-a-half before. The Mets contended again the next two years, but finished third both times. Then, came the tragic day in April 1972, when labor strife was temporarily put aside and the entire baseball world mourned the death of one of its most highly-respected figures.

Many Mets fans felt the club showed bad taste by almost immediately naming coach Yogi Berra as his successor, but the front office felt it was important for organizational continuity. Three days later, the Mets acquired Rusty Staub from Montreal for three of their best prospects (Ken Singleton, Tim Foli, and Mike Jorgensen). Both Staub and Berra made huge contributions to the Mets' winning the 1973 pennant and nearly upsetting the Oakland A's in the World Series. Interestingly, by the end of 1975, they both would also be gone from the organization: Berra would be fired and Staub would be traded. When it was most needed, however, these two immensely popular personalities helped ease the grief of the loss of Gil Hodges, one of baseball's most beloved men.

#5 Low Quality Move—This Local is Now an Express

When the Mets originally began operations in the Spring of 1961, the front office's strategy was to accumulate as many "young arms" as possible while simultaneously appealing to the nostalgic sentiments of former Brooklyn Dodgers and New York Giants fans. They drafted ex-Dodgers Gil Hodges, Roger Craig, and Charlie Neal, former Giant Hobie Landrith, and even dipped into the pool from whence Yankee talent came and acquired Gene Woodling and "Marvelous" Marv Throneberry.

Though the Mets lost far more frequently than they won, it was the ingenious ways they could, as one writer put it, "snatch defeat from the jaws of victory," combined with the preciousness of every comparatively rare triumph that gripped New York fans to their new N.L. team. Improvement was gradual, and the stockpile of hungry hard-throwing pitchers grew steadily. Of all who fit this mold, one stood out far beyond the others: Lynn Nolan Ryan.

Ryan, who prefers to be addressed by his middle moniker, was born in 1947 in Refugio, Texas, and grew up in another nearby small town called Alvin. Future Met teammate Jerry Koosman once quipped, "The town's so small, it doesn't even have a last name." People soon took less interest in the size of his community and more in the rapidity of his velocity. His fastball was being clocked in the Bob Feller range, reputedly around 100 miles per hour. Ryan was also wild enough in his two-plus minor league seasons to walk 200 batters in 291 innings. However, that wildness also worked to his advantage as few hitters were courageous or masochistic enough to hang in there against him, as he struck out 445 and allowed only 183 hits in that same time frame!

Ryan stuck with the team for good in 1968, splitting his time as a spot starter and long reliever, amassing similar hits, walks, and strikeouts to innings ratios as he had in the minors. He was, of course, a key member of the '69 Championship team, going 6-3 during the regular season (with 92 K's in 89 innings), getting the clinching victory of the NLCS in 7 innings of relief, and even securing one of his four career saves in the 3rd game of the World Series. Though still maintaining his excellent strikeout and hit ratios over the next two seasons, the Mets' front office grew weary of his wildness (213 bases-on-balls in 284 innings pitched) and his high ERA's (a composite 3.71 in 1970–1971).

Although Ryan seemed to have shaken the injury jinx that had plagued him earlier in his career (strained muscles, sore elbows, and fingertip blisters which he used to treat by dipping his fingers in pickle brine and rattlesnake venom), the Mets brass finally lost patience. On December 10, 1971, still just a month-and-a-half shy of his 25th birthday, he was shipped with three minor leaguers to the California Angels for shortstop turned third baseman Jim Fregosi.

The deal had an almost identical outcome to the one the Mets had made a little more than two years ago: namely, a "crown jewel" prospect is sent to another team in a much smaller media market and becomes an All-Star, while the over-the-hill veteran infielder the Mets receive falls flat on his face. The trade two years before involved Amos Otis and Joe Foy; now, it's Nolan Ryan and Jim Fregosi.

Ryan immediately establishes himself as the most dominant over-powering pitcher in baseball. He wins 19, has 20 complete games including a league-leading 9 shutouts, fans 329 and secures the best ERA of his major league career so far: 2.28. He even set a record few people know about that still endures: opponents hit a meager .170 batting average against him; and this was only the beginning.

Meanwhile, Fregosi flopped just as badly as Foy had previously done, but was amazingly able to make it to the middle of the next season before being released. In an incredible twist of irony, Fregosi actually wound up becoming Ryan's *manager* for 1¾ seasons, when the Angels hired him 45 games into the 1978 season.

"Ryan's Express," as he was dubbed by Mets' broadcaster Bob Murphy, rolled into high gear in 1973. He achieved 2 no-hitters within a 2-month span, narrowly missed pitching 2 others on different occasions, allowed only 238 hits in 326 innings (although he did walk 162) and broke the single-season strikeout mark formerly held by Sandy Koufax. Going into his final start, Ryan faced the Minnesota Twins 15 shy of tying the standard. Ryan was suffering from the same muscle cramps he used to get in the minor leagues, partially due to the stress of throwing so many pitches during the season and also because of the pressure being placed on him. Nolan gutted it out, and when the game went into extra innings, he both tied and broke Koufax's record. The Angels even won the game for him, giving him 21 victories, a new personal best.

He won 22 more the next year (which would be his career high) and fanned 367, amassing a mind-boggling 3 consecutive seasons aggregate total of 1,079, another record that's been challenged but has stood the test of time. He found the opportunity to pitch 2 more no-hitters over the ensuing 2 seasons, tying Koufax as the paramount no-hit hurler. Ryan even bettered Koufax in a way: Nolan pitched his 4 "no-no's" in a 3-year period, while it took Sandy 4. However, there are two "mountains" Koufax did climb that Ryan never could quite reach the summits. One was pitching a perfect game, which Koufax accomplished September 9, 1965 vs. the Chicago Cubs. The other was winning the Cy Young Award; in fact, Koufax's winning it three times (in '63, '65, and '66) was all the more impressive since at the time only one award was given covering both the American and National Leagues. Also Koufax was pitching in tremendous pain his last two seasons, suffering from an arthritic elbow, decided not to risk crippling himself and retired after the 1966 World Series and just before his 31st birthday.

Luckily, and greatly due to his rigorous physical fitness regimen, Ryan was not faced with such a decision until he was in his mid-40's! Just as he had been a cornerstone of the Mets' change for the better, Ryan played the same role for the Angels during the 1970's and, after losing out to the Oakland Athletics and then the Kansas City Royals, they were finally able to win the A.L. Western Division title in 1979. Ironically, his last game as an Angel would be his start in the opener of the ALCS vs. Baltimore. Ryan gave up only 1 run and 4 hits in 7 innings, but left the game with a no-decision. The Orioles would go on to win the game in extra innings (on John Lowenstein's pinch-hit three-run homer) and also defeat the Angels in four games, clinching their first pennant in 8 years.

Feeling he'd carried the team as long as he could and leaving them in seemingly "smooth" straits, Ryan had always had the desire to pitch close to home in Texas. The Houston Astros made Nolan's decision even easier by offering him a 9-year, $15 million veteran free-agent contract, which at the time made him the highest paid athlete in the U.S.A. He gave the Astros and their fans more than their money's worth in terms of productivity and excitement and drawing power.

He led them to "2½" division titles: two "full" titles in 1980 and 1986, and one "half" title in 1981, in which Houston lost the extra-scheduled round of playoffs to the Los Angeles Dodgers brought about by the mid-summer's players strike. In 1980, he had the Astros' on the very precipice of their first pennant, as they were six outs away from victory with a three-run advantage in the fifth and deciding contest. Incredibly, the Astros blew the lead and, although they eventually tied the game, the Philadelphia Phillies won it in extra innings to clinch *their* first pennant in *thirty* years.

Ryan had long since surpassed Walter Johnson's record strikeout total of 3,508 when, in July 1985, poised to set a new milestone, he faced the team who had originally nurtured him, the Mets. To add to the irony, he achieved his

4,000[th] strikeout vs. former teammate Danny Heep, for whom the Mets had also traded a young pitching prospect several years before: Mike Scott. The following season, Scott would win the N.L. Cy Young Award (an honor which, as previously mentioned, eluded Ryan), pitch a no-hitter to clinch the N.L. Western Division title, and even be selected M.V.P. of the NLCS. The unfortunate circumstance, as far as Ryan and the Astros were concerned, was that the New York Mets, who had a franchise-record 108 victories that year, added 4 more in the playoffs. Although Ryan pitched for 7 more seasons, he never appeared in the post-season again. In fact, his lone championship ring came from the '69 Miracle Mets.

Before one starts to feel too sorry for him, remember that he won 2 ERA and 2 strikeout titles in his tenure with Houston, finally broke another of Koufax's records by pitching his fifth no-hitter, and when his contract expired in 1988, he played out his option and signed with the Texas Rangers. In 1989, he became the oldest hurler to fan 300 batters in a season, while securing his 11th of his (another record) 12 "K" titles. The next year, he not only got his 300th career victory, he also pitched his sixth no-hitter, vs. the defending World Champion Oakland A's. The "cherry on the sundae" came the following season, when at age 44, he twirled his 7th no-hitter. He finally retired in 1993 nearly 1,600 whiffs ahead of his closest competitor. In 1999, in a poll of sportswriters and fans, he was named the right-handed starting pitcher on the All-Century Team.

#6 Combined High & Low Quality Move—"The Say Hey Kid"

Arguably the best and most popular player that was lost to New York fans after the Dodgers and Giants en masse exodus after the '57 season was Willie Mays. He was a black player who was a favorite of fans of all races and creeds, mostly due to his seeming child-like exuberance for the game, combined with his tremendous all-around talent. During the "Golden Age" of New York baseball, from 1951–57, the debate raged about who was the greatest centerfielder in the game: Willie Mays, Mickey Mantle, or Duke Snider? Other clubs boasted fine centerfielders in their own right during that era, i.e. Richie Ashburn of the Phillies, Larry Doby of the Indians, Gus Bell of the Reds, Bill Bruton of the Braves, and Jimmy Piersall of the Red Sox, to name the "best of the rest."

However, the centerfield position was dominated for the vast majority of the '50's by the triumvirate of New Yorkers, made even more famous years later in a lyrical manner by songwriter Terry Cashman: "Willie, Mickey, and the Duke." The self-proclaimed balladeer of baseball forever immortalized these three great players, and while the argument still goes on today among fans and experts over which of them was the greatest, there is little argument that they share the pantheon all to themselves.

In terms of overall success, Mantle wins the dispute hands down. The Yankees won 6 pennants and 4 World Series in that span, and he had much to do with it. He won the A.L. Most Valuable Player Award twice, the Triple Crown once (leading in batting average, home runs, and RBI all in the same season), accumulated 207 homers, 669 RBI, scored 763 runs, walked 670 times, and amassed a .316 batting average. Under World Series pressure, Mantle more than held his own: in the six times the Yanks were in the Series, not counting the '51 Series, which he missed most of due to an unfortunate spill in the outfield, "The Commerce Comet" smacked 9 homers (half his career Series total), scored 18 runs, drove in 17, and despite batting only .264, he made most of his hits "long" ones and toted up 58 total bases for a slugging percentage of .547!

"The Dook of Flatbush" need not take a backseat to anyone, nor does he have to make excuses for playing half his games in such a hitter-friendly park as Ebbets Field, where the greatest fence distance was 390 feet from home plate. In fact, Snider actually hit the exact number of homers in the five consecutive seasons ('53–'57) he hit 40 or more as Mantle had in the entire 7 years: 207. Add the 29 Snider hit in '51 and the 21 in '52 and he's got "The Mick" beaten by a wide margin. Snider had other statistics comparable or better than Mantle's, including being the only player in baseball history to hit 4 home runs in a single World Series on two different occasions ('52 & '55, when the Brooks won their only championship). Snider was also a great defensive outfielder who knew how to play the quirky caroms of Ebbets' walls and screens. Mantle signed as a shortstop, and even if he hadn't proven himself hazardous to the health of anyone sitting in the vicinity of first base (either the dugout or the stands), it's doubtful Mantle would ever have stuck as a shortstop, since the Yankees already had both Phil Rizzuto and Gil McDougald manning the position. What Mantle lacked in grace, he more than made up for in speed and the centerfield at Yankee Stadium that was Death Valley-esque proved advantageous as, before Mantle's legs betrayed him, he could outrun any fly ball.

Nevertheless, the one who most experts agreed was the greatest of them all was "The Say Hey Kid," Willie Mays. As his former manager Leo Durocher once said, Mays was by the far the best "five-tool" player: he could hit for average, he could hit for power, he could run (on both the bases paths and in the field), he could throw extremely well, and he could "go get 'em" on defense. It isn't completely fair to compare Willie to Mickey or Duke strictly on statistics, since he had missed nearly two full seasons to military duty in Korea between the ages of 21 and 22. However, when Mays returned to the Giants in 1954, he more than made up for lost time, leading the N.L. in batting (.345), slugging (.667), and triples (13), while finishing 2nd in total bases (377), runs (119), and tied for 3rd in both hits (195) and home runs (41). More importantly, his first M.V.P. season helped lead the Giants to the pennant and to an incredible four-game sweep in the World Series over the immensely favored Cleveland Indians. Of course, what most baseball fans talk about to this day (due to it being one of the most replayed sequences in sports history) was the marvelous catch Mays made in the 8th inning of the Series' opener at the PoloGrounds. Left-handed relief pitcher Don Liddle had just been brought into the game specifically to face Cleveland's left-handed hitting first baseman Vic Wertz with runners on first and second, nobody out, and a 2-2 score.

Liddle always joked that he got Wertz to hit the ball exactly where he wanted him to: nearly 480 feet away to dead center. Fortunately, Liddle had Mays patrolling the area and after a long sprint, he caught the ball over his left shoulder on the warning track, with his back to the infield. In one fluid motion, Mays spun on his heel and heaved the ball back towards the cutoff man behind second base, allowing only the runner from second to advance. This was considered the turning point of the Series, as the Indians did not score, the game went into extra innings and the Giants won on James "Dusty" Rhodes' three-run pinch-hit homer (on which Mays scored the winning run). All aspects of the Indians normally sound fundamentals fell apart after that. They wound up posting an ERA over two points higher than their regular season league-leading 2.78. They hit only two home runs after also leading the A.L. with 156; they even committed four errors while they posted the second best fielding percentage during what was their dream season of 1954 until the New York Giants, led by Willie Mays, turned it into a nightmare.

Unfortunately, this is the only time Mays would be able to win a Championship, but that didn't stop him from having a stellar career. The next season, he again led the league in triples and slugging, but instead of a batting title, he paced the N.L. with his first of two 50-homer seasons (finishing with 51). Perhaps the biggest on-the-field setback of his life occurred at the end of that year when Leo Durocher, his mentor who had stuck by him when he struggled as a rookie and had been a surrogate father, resigned as manager. Mays had such love and respect for Durocher that he always referred to him as "Missa" (which, of course, meant "Mister") Leo, as Willie never completely lost his Alabama drawl. This was one of the attributes that attracted fans, particularly the relatively cosmopolitan fans of New York. Willie was a black Southerner and although he lacked formal education (playing in the Negro Leagues at the age of 13 didn't leave much time for school), he was highly intelligent and articulate. He had good basic business acumen and, with the help of teammate and future manager Herman Franks, was able to invest his money from baseball and perquisites such as endorsements wisely. Unfortunately, a few years later, he became vulnerable to leeches looking to cash in on The Say Hey Kid's name and fortune, including his first wife, who had a reputation for being a free spender. This eventually led to a bitter divorce and child custody battle.

In the meantime, Willie was still setting new baseball standards. In 1956, he became the first "30-30" player, hitting over thirty homers (36) and stealing over

30 bases (40) in the same season. The following year, he hit possibly the pinnacle of his tenure as a New York Giant when he became the second player (and one of only four in major league history) to collect at least 20 doubles, 20 triples, and 20 homers concurrently. He had also his second consecutive 30-30 season and for the third time in four years, led the N.L. in slugging percentage (.626). However, Willie and all his fans were dealt, as The Bard would say, "the unkindest cut of all," when in 1958, the Giants were playing their home games a continent away to the West, at Seals Stadium in San Francisco. Willie continued his exemplary production in his new "digs," batting over .300 for seven straight seasons (carrying over from '57 and lasting till '63), while smashing more than 30 homers a year in a different stretch ('61 to '66, including his career high of 52 in '65, while winning his 2nd N.L. M.V.P. Award), leading the league in runs twice, stolen bases twice, and slugging twice, and in bases-on-balls once.

He accomplished all this while calling Candlestick Park home, in which the swirling winds off of Candlestick Point by San Francisco Bay almost always blew from leftfield toward rightfield, which was a definite detriment to a right-handed batter. However, Willie being the "student of the game" that he was, adjusted and was able to use the unfavorable conditions to his advantage and drive balls to right-center, without altering his normal swing. This enabled him to hit a major league lifetime total of 660 homers, which is currently third on the all time list, but is being vigorously challenged by Mays' own godson, Barry Bonds. The protégé of Mays' former S.F. teammate, Bobby Bonds, is also the only other member (besides Willie) of the "600-300" club: 600 homers and 300 steals. The younger Bonds just recently established his own yardstick by which all future slugger/speedsters will be measured: "600-500"; and while "pushing" 40 as of this writing, he's still going strong. Bonds gives credit to both his father and godfather in so far as teaching him fundamentals, work habits, and physical and mental conditioning.

While Mays played his heart out for the Bay Area fans, he was never fully accepted to their proverbial bosom the way "native" talent such as Orlando Cepeda, Juan Marichal, and Willie McCovey were. Many blamed him for the Giants' inability to win more than 1 pennant (in '62) and no World Championships. Then in a four-year period, Mays' stats began to decline, by *his* lofty standards. From 1967–1970, he accrued "only" 86 homers, 325 runs, 290 RBI, 29 steals (between the ages of 36–39), and batted a "mere" .282, numbers that in today's market, players would be clamoring for multi-million dollar, multi-year contracts. Mays had one last hurrah with the Giants in 1971, helping lead them to the N.L. Western Division title, and in a reversal of roles, the Giants almost blew a big lead in the standings and had to hold off a furious rush by the Los Angeles Dodgers, winning by just a single game. Willie could not, however, prevent San Francisco from being defeated in the NLCS by the Pittsburgh Pirates, despite his 2 doubles, 1 homer, 1 stolen base, and 3 RBI in 15 at bats in the four games. Again, the fans and the media unjustly vilified him, and this intensified his desire to go elsewhere.

The following spring, Willie showed his true character when he refused to cross the picket line of the MLBPA strike, and encouraged all other players to abide by his example. It was in this arena that Mays, who by this time was the elder statesman of players, although not a union player representative, held court and his compatriots followed suit. Within days, the *owners* broke ranks and the strike was settled in a relatively expedient manner. One of the victories the players secured was the "10 and 5 rule," which stipulates that any player with a minimum of ten years of major league service and at least five consecutive seasons with the same club may *not* be traded without his approval. This also proved great leverage for players *wanting* to be traded, as had been the case with Willie. Before this rule, Mays could have been sent to any major league team. Now, he was able to choose where he wished to go to: the Mets.

Willie's wish, and the dream of millions of New York baseball fans came true on May 11, 1972 when The Say Hey Kid "came home", being acquired for pitcher Charlie Williams. Although the Mets had gotten off to a terrific start, winning 18 of their first 25 games, the bitter taste of the players strike and the collective grief of Gil Hodges' sudden catastrophic passing away had left a pall over the entire organization. Few other additions to the team could have given the Mets a greater injection of energy; in fact, Mrs. Payson, the club's principal owner, had publicly avowed that she had long desired for Willie to finish out his brilliant career where he started. Of course, now she would most likely be brought up on "tampering" charges; but, at the time (as still is the case), she was merely echoing the sentiments of a lot of New York fans, not just Mets' followers. It's very doubtful Mays would have ever wound up in *Yankee* pinstripes; not that the "Bronx Bomber" organization or fans wouldn't have welcomed him, but with the waiver restrictions (especially at that time), such a transaction was almost impossible.

Willie's debut three days after his acquisition came on not only at a Shea Stadium Ladies' Day promotion for Mother's Day, but against his former club, the Giants. Willie, despite being a bit choked up by the overwhelming standing ovation his first time up, and the prospect of opposing his former teammates, some of whom he had played with quite a long time, rose to the occasion with his usual flair, slamming a 5th inning homer to break a 4-4 tie and ultimately winning the game for his *new* mates. The Mets were in the midst of a team-record tying eleven-game winning streak and were able to hold first place in the N.L. East well into June. Then, injuries began mounting, and although their pitching remained intact (Tom Seaver won 21 games with 249 K's, Tug McGraw had 27 saves, and Jon Matlack's 15 victories were good enough to ensure his selection as N.L. Rookie-of-the-Year), not one Met regular collected 100 hits and the club sank into third place, finishing 13½ games behind Pittsburgh. To his credit, Mays did what he could to contribute, hitting 8 homers, scoring 35, driving in 22 and splitting his 69 games as a Met playing centerfield (after Tommie Agee's injury and subsequent release), or platooning at first base, and batting .364 as a pinch hitter. Again, his intangible qualities shone through and Willie's very presence hugely benefited the club, regardless of statistics.

Unfortunately, Willie's age and the wear and tear of 28 professional seasons (including Negro Leagues, minor leagues, and N.L. service) made even *him* susceptible to the injury bug and in 1973, he saw action in only 66 games, in which he could only muster 6 homers, 25 RBI, and an anemic .211 batting average. Many other Mets were on the disabled list and the club languished in last place for most of the season. In June, he publicly announced he planned to retire at season's end; he probably would've quit much sooner than that, but his loyalty to the club, not wanting to seem like he was bailing out of a sinking ship, and, like just about anybody else, needing his salary prevailed upon him to finish out the year. The club rewarded him by not releasing him, partly out of goodwill and partly out of necessity, since Willie, although he was far from being healthy, was still a "warm body" that the Mets could sometimes put on the field.

The National League also showed somewhat uncharacteristic class by including him on their roster for the All-Star Game in Kansas City on July 24. Facing Yankees' ace reliever Albert "Sparky" Lyle in the eighth inning, Willie came up as pinch-hitter, receiving an ovation from the fans at Royals Stadium, which is a true testament to his legacy. Even after he struck out on 3 pitches, the cheering continued for several minutes.

That was nothing compared to the ovations he got two months and a day later at Shea Stadium on "Willie Mays Night." The occasion was emotional enough; the Mets had planned it upon Mays' retirement announcement for a mid-week night game vs. the Montreal Expos, figuring it would otherwise be a meaningless "mop-up" game. Little did the front office realize how amazingly (there's no better way to put it, although that adjective has become overused in club lore) the Mets would rally and be in the midst of a pennant race. Thus, the park was SRO, as many former New York baseball legends, including "Mickey & the Duke" paid homage to Willie in a pregame ceremony. Mays himself delivered an emotional speech, which was barely audible to the overflowing crowd, who would not stop chanting his name, perhaps cathartically in apology for the way he had never been fully appreciated by San Francisco after he was literally ripped from New York in his prime. Lou Gehrig's famous "Luckiest man on the face of the Earth" farewell speech is in a reliquary all by itself; nevertheless, Willie's conclusion of his own speech deserves consideration for similar veneration: "Willie, say good-bye to America." While his plight was not anywhere nearly as dire as Gehrig's, the similarity was that he was forced to step down from the profession he loved and exhibited more skill than most ever had because his body would no longer allow him to continue.

Incredibly, Mays' playing career still had an epilogue to it. The Mets won the N.L. Eastern Division by 1½ games and split the first four games of the NLCS with the Cincinnati Reds. In the 10th inning of the 4th contest, rightfielder Rusty Staub had made a spectacular game-saving catch (right out of Willie Mays' own repertoire) but had crashed into the then-unpadded rightfield wall and separated his right shoulder. When the Mets lost in the 12th on Pete Rose's solo homer and a 5th game was necessary and Reds' righty ace Jack Billingham was slated to pitch, the Mets were forced to start Ed Kranepool in Staub's stead. Kranepool drove in the Mets' first two runs, but the Reds tied the score. It was still 2-2 in the 5th when the Mets' magic surfaced as they caught an unexpected break. Wayne Garrett led off with a double and when Felix Millan laid down a poor sacrifice bunt, Billingham threw to third base in plenty of time to nail Garrett. However, rookie third baseman Dan Driessen (who in later years would play a key role in the Reds' back-to-back Championships in '75 & '76), this time "pulled a rock" and didn't tag Garrett, thinking there was a force on. The Reds then came apart at the seams, much in the manner the Mets had been notorious for, allowing a double and a walk, giving the Mets a two-run lead, reloading the bases, and knocking Billingham out of the box.

After the Reds' left-handed starter from Game 2, Don Gullett, had walked John Milner and was scheduled to face Kranepool, the ballpark by Flushing Bay was sent into delirium as Willie Mays made his first appearance of the playoffs as a pinch-hitter. When Cincinnati skipper George "Sparky" Anderson countered with his right-handed ace reliever Clay Carroll, Mets' manager Yogi Berra decided to let Mays bat anyway, mostly again out of necessity. Willie, in his 22 seasons, plus 4 previous post-season encounters had totaled 1,329 extra-base hits, but the dribbler he slapped up the third-base line in this at bat was as important a safety as he'd ever marshaled in his whole life. It went for an RBI single, and he eventually came around to score as the Mets put the game out of reach, 7-2, and won a pennant even more improbable than the "Miracle Mets" of '69.

Staub was still in tremendous pain for the outset of the World Series, so manager Berra tried reaching into his "bag of tricks" once more and gave Willie the start in centerfield for the lid lifter vs. the Oakland A's southpaw Ken Holtzman. Unfortunately, it was simply a case of the "spirit being willing, but the flesh being lacking." Willie was not up to the task, especially in the spacious and sun-drenched outfield of the Oakland Alameda Coliseum. Mays made one official error, misplayed several others, and was further embarrassed when he stumbled and fell attempting to make a catch that even several years earlier he would have made with ease. As one cynical sarcastic scribe was loath enough to write, "Mays went from a basket catcher to a basket case." He did have one last "brief shining moment" in Game 2, driving in the winning run with a ground single up the middle. He had another single and scored one run in his seven at bats, but was deliberately *not* used by Berra in the middle of a last-inning desperation rally in Game 7. Mets' broadcaster Ralph Kiner, a Hall-of-Fame player who ironically had to prematurely retire due to a back injury, was in the Mets' clubhouse interviewing the team after the defeat. He remarked that Mays looked like "The Portrait of Dorian Gray," as the pressure and rigors of playing baseball nearly three decades had taken its toll all at once.

The aftermath of Mays' playing career should have been happy, but real life is rarely like fantasy. The Mets employed Mays as a coach for several years, although there was really no place on their staff for him, and this was before major league teams carried bench coaches and hitting instructors. Mays was still in shaky financial shape, so this was the best alternative, since neither the Mets nor any other organization offered him a position either in the front office or as a manager at any level. In 1979, the year Mays was enshrined in the Hall-of-Fame (naturally on his first try), he was hired as a spokesman for Bally's Casino in Atlantic City. He had accepted this (as too had fellow legend Mickey Mantle, to whom Mays seemed inexorably linked) merely to supplement his income and *not* to promote gambling or detract appeal to baseball. However, MLB decided that both Mantle and Mays were involved in a conflict of interest and had to either resign from Bally's or be excluded from any baseball operations. When all major league organizations refused to match the money they were making in Atlantic City, both opted for the latter. It is a sad coda for these men that, although both Mantle and Mays were eventually reinstated, they ultimately had to renounce their association with the business they had helped make so popular. They both deserved better treatment.

#7 Combined High & Low Quality Move—"LeGrand Orange"

There is no other way to put it: the New York Mets desired Daniel Joseph Staub ever since he was a red-headed, freckle-faced teenager, and in an almost celestial manner, stepped right out of the pages of "Archie Comics." "Rusty," as he was affectionately known, was also coveted by the other 19 major league baseball teams while still a high school star in Latrop, a suburb of New Orleans, Louisiana. The left-handed hitting, right-handed throwing outfielder (who occasionally played first base or catcher) was paradoxically a throwback and neologist in terms of being a ball-player. As far as his ability to "stick to tradition," he always swung a heavier than normal weighted bat and choked up a couple of inches on the handle. This did not cut down on his power as he blasted 291 homers in his 23-year career, including a personal best of 30 in 1970. On the contrary, it made him all the more dangerous hitter against all types of pitching, as he was able to drive the ball equally adeptly from "foul line to foul line."

He was also a pioneer in the development and use of batting gloves. There were some major leaguers who used golf gloves, especially on the hand that was closest to the knob of the bat, mostly to prevent blisters due to the torque the "bottom" hand has to endure when swinging a bat. However, none of the companies associated with baseball equipment, such as Spalding or Rawlings, had ever designed a glove specifically intended for baseball hitters' benefit. Unfortunately, a machismo attitude still prevailed among many associated with baseball that the utilization of batting gloves was "sissy" or "unmanly," much the way batting helmets were perceived for a long time. Luckily, Staub was brilliant and thick-skinned enough to ignore the pundits and actually "built a better mousetrap," not completely changing the golf glove, but merely altering it so its protective principles could be adjusted for baseball. Perhaps employing a bit of psychological warfare, Staub also used a variety of colors, usually dark shades. This was to give an air of intimidation and often worked. Staub experienced his quota of "chin music" and "bench-jockeying" because of his insight, but he managed to consistently succeed where many others had failed and, as the saying goes, "had the last laugh."

Staub graduated from high school in 1962 and mused many college scholarships (he was an accomplished football and basketball player) but was also shrewd enough to realize that he could demand a big contract from any baseball team. He also realized that signing with one of the new expansion teams would exponentially hasten his ascension to the major league level. The bidding wars that went on between teams for high school (and in some instances college) stars inevitably led to the free agent draft, which was instituted three years later in 1965. This enables teams with poorer records and less money than their competitors to get first opportunity at being able to sign better quality players in order to improve their chances of contending. Staub had narrowed down to where he wanted to sign to three teams: the St. Louis Cardinals, the Los Angeles Angels, and the Houston Colt .45's. All were desperate for young talent.

The Cardinals, although not an expansion team, had not won the N.L. pennant since 1946 and had finished "out of the money" (fourth place or lower) 7 of the last 12 years. Also, like many fans growing up in Louisiana, Staub had been a Cardinal follower as their T.V. & radio broadcasts reached all around the South. However, the Cardinals already had an established outfield of Stan "The Man" Musial, Curt Flood, and Charlie James, and within two years, would literally "steal" Lou Brock from the Chicago Cubs.

First base was not a viable option either, as Bill White solidly manned that position, with rookie Fred Whitfield backing him up, if only for that season. Thus, as attractive as the prospect might have been, those factors eliminated St. Louis from Rusty's plans.

The Angels were also an appealing option as they were only in their second year in the A.L., had finished a very respectable 8th in a 10-team league, only 21 games under .500, played in a very hitter-friendly stadium, Wrigley Park, and offered "extra-curricular" incentives (such as endorsements) that few other markets could match. Incredibly, Staub faced the same obstacles as in St. Louis: other players already being established at the positions he'd be vying for. The Angels had a substantial core of outfielders including Leon Wagner, Earl Averill Jr., Albie Pearson, and George Thomas. As far as being a "first sacker", the Angels had a platoon of Lee Thomas and Steve Bilko. So it seemed the most logical choice for Rusty was to sign with the Houston club; this way he would have the least competition and the quickest path to the majors. Colt .45's' owner Judge Roy Hofheinz heartily agreed and signed Staub to a bonus contract.

Staub was also happy to be given the chance to play close to home, Houston being only around 250 miles from New Orleans, and at the time, was the closest franchise to "The Big Easy." Nonetheless, Rusty would still have to spend some time on "Tobacco Road," as he was sent to the Colt .45's Durham affiliate in the Carolina League. Staub quickly proved he made the right decision as in 140 games as Durham's first baseman, he socked 23 homers, drove in 93, scored 115, batted .293, slugged .483, and even stole 9 bases. He was brought up for a "cup of coffee" at the tail end of the season, but never even "got to the urn." No matter: Staub would be "earning" plenty for years to come, as the next season, he made the Colt .45's as a 19-year old phenom.

As a rookie, he split his 150 games between the outfield (105) and first base (45), and switching positions several times whenever Manager Harry Craft (whom Staub greatly respected) determined a double switch was necessary. Rusty struggled, however, batting only .224 with 6 homers and 45 RBI. In fairness, besides being a relative neophyte learning his way around major league pitching (arguably the toughest in the world), the entire National League only batted .245 and had a composite ERA of 3.29! Batters were in the midst of what some baseball experts call "The Second Dead Ball Era." There were several contributing factors: the height of the mound was 15 inches, most ballparks either already were pitching-oriented or on their way to becoming that way, and some of the greatest pitchers of all time were in their primes. Dominant hurlers such as Sandy Koufax, Juan Marichal, Whitey Ford, Bob Gibson, Gary Peters, Gaylord Perry, Camilo Pascual, Dean Chance, Mickey Lolich, and, yes, lest we forget, Denny McLain, made it difficult for hitters to earn a living until the mound's elevation was reduced to 10 inches in 1969. Until then, pitchers literally "had the upper hand."

Meanwhile, Staub's "growing pains" continued as he hit only .216 in 89 games and was finally demoted to Oklahoma City of the Pacific Coast League. Many others might have sulked or even given up, but Rusty again showed his mettle and literally tore up the P.C.L., batting .314 with 20 homers and 45 RBI, averaging a hit a game for his 71 contests. The following spring, not only did Staub finally stick with the parent club for good, but he was able to help "christen" the 8th Wonder of the World: the Astrodome.

The "Dome" turned out to be perhaps the worst hitters park in major league history. Despite having Astroturf installed in its second year (because the grass died when the roof had to be blackened out due to the sunlight making it dangerous to field fly balls), which made grounders speed through the infield, even well-stroked drives that would have gone for long hits in any other stadium literally died in the Astrodome's heavy air-conditioned atmosphere. Although faced with this additional handicap, Staub still produced well for the Astros (their new name to suit their new arena), hitting a composite .292 for the next four seasons, with 43 homers and 290 RBI, excellent numbers for the cavernous "Dome." 1967 was his best season, leading the majors in doubles with 44 and finishing fifth in the N.L. in batting at .333, 7 percentage points higher than A.L. Triple Crown winner Carl Yastrzemski. The Astros had been steadily improving and adding a nucleus of some fine talent around Staub (such as Joe Morgan, Jimmy Wynn, Denis Menke, Bob Aspromonte, Larry Dierker, and Mike Cuellar) and seemed to be on the verge of genuine contention. Fate had other plans in store for the Astros, and it all started in a kitchen of the Hotel Ambassador in Los Angeles, seemingly a universe removed from the Astrodome and the baseball world.

On June 5, 1968, minutes after he declared victory in the California State Primary, while in the midst of what seemed to be a successful campaign to win the nomination for the Presidential candidacy of the Democratic Party, Senator Robert F. Kennedy was shot and mortally wounded by an assassin. He was pronounced dead early the next morning, eliciting horrific memories from only two months ago when popular civil rights leader Dr. Martin Luther King was gunned down in Memphis and the opening of the baseball season was delayed out of necessity, due to the mass rioting in the aftermath. MLB Commissioner William Eckert decreed no games would be postponed, however, any player may "pay respects" by taking a personal hiatus on participation in games scheduled for the day of Senator Kennedy's funeral, June 8th. Most players declined this offer, but Rusty Staub did not. He had been a great admirer of both Senator Kennedy and his slain brother, President John F. Kennedy, and took the opportunity to show it. Although his action was sanctioned by both the Commissioner of Baseball and the President of the United States, Lyndon Johnson (who had declared a national day of mourning), Staub's "sentimentality" did not sit well with Astros' management. Mostly because of this philosophical disagreement, Staub was left unprotected in the upcoming Expansion Draft and wound up "property of the Montreal Expos." Still only 25, he quickly secured himself the star and most popular player of his new club, batting .302, smacking 29 homers with 79 RBI, and tying for third in the N.L. in walks with 110.

Houston, meanwhile, started the season in a dreadful manner with a 4-20 record and was no-hit by Jim Maloney of the Cincinnati Reds at Crosley Field to finish their horrid month of April. Fiery Donald Wilson took May Day literally and returned the favor by hurling a no-hitter at the Reds, winning 4-0, and waking the Astros out of their sleepwalking. They actually contended for a time, getting as close as 2½ games out of first place, but they had dug themselves too big a hole and wound up 5th in the newly devised N.L. Western Division, but breaking even at 81-81. This is where many superstitious baseball fans believe "The Curse of LeGrand Orange" may have begun.

Many Boston Red Sox followers firmly believe in "The Curse of the Bambino," which originated when Babe Ruth was sold to the New York Yankees in 1920. The Red Sox had won the World Series 4 times between 1912–1918, but have not done it since, despite winning the A.L. pennant four times. Each time, they've made it to the seventh game ('46, '67, '75, & '86) only to lose each time in heart-wrenching fashion. As of this writing, the Yankees, over the same time period since *acquiring* Ruth for what would still be considered a "nice chunk o'change," have won 26 World Series and 39 A.L. pennants!

"The Curse of LeGrand Orange" may be a milder hex by comparison, but many Astros' fans believe it exists. Upon his arrival in Montreal, which happens to be in the French Canadian province of Quebec, Rusty was dubbed "LeGrand Orange," which simply means "The Big Orange," or can be loosely translated to "Big Red." Thus, Staub had such immediate success in his new environment (despite the chillier weather conditions), Jarry Park being more hitter-friendly than Colts Stadium or the Astrodome ever were. Staub's flourishing career, combined with the fact that the Astros got almost nothing in return for him while they continue to flounder (having never won the N.L. pennant, again as of this writing), has even the most intellectual Astros fans believing in a curse. Staub hit 78 homers, drove in 270, scored 281, walked 296 times, batted .296, slugged .501, and even found time, despite his reputation for "lack of nimbleness" on the base paths, to steal 24 bases in three full seasons North of the Border. He was voted to the All-Star Team all three times, and was selected 2nd team all-N.L. twice.

Then, during the ensuing baseball strike, perhaps due to his high profile union activities, Staub was traded to the New York Mets for their aforementioned top prospects: Ken Singleton, Tim Foli, and Mike Jorgensen. If, as the saying goes, "Misery loves company," then Astros' fans suddenly found themselves with another group of fans that were commiserating with them. It's not that the three men Montreal obtained for Staub didn't produce; both Singleton and Foli eventually became All-Stars. It's just that it seemed like another team gave up on Staub too quickly and he was more than happy to make them pay for it. Rusty got off to a good start with the Mets in 1972, and, as has also been previously mentioned, helped the entire Mets organization get over the shock of losing highly popular and beloved manager Gil Hodges. Unfortunately, the day the world celebrated the 3rd anniversary of the first moon landing, July 20th, Rusty was struck by a *different* missile: a fastball from future teammate southpaw George Stone, whom Braves' manager Lum Harris had inserted into the game specifically to pitch to Staub. Both Stone and Staub insist that the brush-back pitch was not intended to cause injury, but the result was still a fracture in one of the bones in Rusty's right hand, putting him on the disabled list for the first time in his entire career. Again, many players would have "folded their tents" and said "Sayonara!" for the season, but Rusty rehabilitated and came back for September. Knowledgeable New York fans (there's *that* cliché again) appreciate Staub's effort and cheered him despite finishing with only 9 homers and 38 RBI. Staub did hit .293 with a .452 slugging average, so that definitely showed signs of encouragement and reassured Mets' fans that management had *not* pulled an "Otis" or a "Ryan," trading premium prospects for a decrepit veteran. By the end of next year, Staub would justify their faith and confidence, in spades.

In the off-season, the Mets completed one of the best deals in their entire history: they traded pitchers Gary Gentry and Danny Frisella to the Atlanta Braves for second baseman Felix Millan and pitcher George Stone, the same lefthander who had "plunked" Staub the year before. While Gentry and Frisella both developed sore arms, Millan led the team in runs (82), in games played (153), in batting (.290) and set a new team record for hits in a season (185) [he himself broke his own record in '75 with 191 and which stood until '96]. Using his "choke-up to the trademark" batting stance, he also led all of baseball in strikeouts to at bats ratio (22 to 638, for a .967 average of making contact). Millan also solidified the infield, making only 9 errors in 830 chances for a .989 fielding percentage, good for 3rd in the National League, while turning 99 double plays.

Staub undoubtedly felt safer now that Stone was his teammate, and he eventually considered himself lucky, as did the Mets, to have a reliable fourth starter who was 12-3 with a 2.80 earned run average in 27 games. Staub himself also had a fabulous year, leading the team in doubles (36), RBI (76), and walks (74), finishing 2nd on the squad in games played (152), homers (15), hits (163), runs (77), batting average (.279) and slugging percentage (.421). Combine that with Tom Seaver's Cy Young Award performance (a 19-10 record with a league-leading 2.08 ERA, 18 complete games and 251 K's) and one would have thought that the Mets should've been able to run away with the division. However, the injury "bug" that infested the team the previous year was now a "swarm" as virtually everyone else on the roster fell victim to some type of ailment.

Two of the strangest incidents happened at Shea Stadium, which one journalist once described as "the Mets' private torture chamber," due to the swirling winds and the noise of nearby LaGuardia Airport. This time, conversely, the tables were turned and it was the Mets who were "taken out" by the ballpark. In May, Jon Matlack was struck on the forehead by a line drive after delivering a pitch, evoking horrifying memories of when another promising lefthander, Herb Score, had his career severely curtailed after being hit in the eye in an identical fashion. Matlack suffered a hairline skull fracture and many people were ready to write him off the season. Incredibly, he was never put onto the disabled list and returned in a fortnight and resumed his role as their Number 2 starter.

The other more freakish accident occurred in July and did have a far more unfortunate outcome. Centerfielder Don Hahn and rightfielder George "the Stork" Theodore (playing on a day Staub was being rested) were both pursuing a line drive in the right centerfield gap, but between the loud shouting of the crowd and the roar of the overhead airplane, neither could hear the other calling for the ball. The result was a tremendous collision, an inside-the-park homer for the batter, bruised ribs for Hahn, and a dislocated hip for Theodore. "The Stork," as many bench warmers do in New York, had developed a fan following, including a girls' fan club called "The Storkettes." Unlike his namesake, Theodore was unable to play standing on one leg, but for a while it seemed the whole team was playing in poor health. Others such as Cleon Jones, Jerry Grote, John Milner, Bud Harrelson, and even Willie Mays were among the "walking wounded."

Astoundingly, as previously mentioned, the Mets were able to gather their forces, and after going 20-8 in September, clinched the N.L. East the first day of October with only an 82-79 record, still the worst ever for a division winner. In the playoffs vs. Cincinnati, Staub had only 3 hits but they were all homers, good for 5 RBI, 4 runs scored, and an .800 slugging percentage. Few fans will remember his hitting compared to the catch he made to snuff a Reds' rally in Game 4, when he ran full-tilt towards right-center with reckless abandon. However, instead of colliding with a teammate, he crashed into the fence, lay prostrate spread-eagle and barely conscious, but held onto the ball. Had this happened in *this* day and age, the wall would have been cushioned to reduce these kinds of mishaps, and Staub would have had a horse-collar placed around his neck to immobilize his spine (preventing possible paralysis), and he'd have been carted off on a stretcher. Instead, Rusty just laid there until his head cleared (after getting smelling salts from trainer Tom McKenna), was helped to his feet and walked off the field on his own power. Unfortunately, he could not continue in the game and the Mets subsequently lost on Pete Rose's 12th inning homer (exacting a bit of revenge for the way he was pelted by disorderly rowdies after his fight with Bud Harrelson the day before). The worst news was that Staub's right shoulder was separated, and although the Mets managed to win the deciding game the next day, Rusty's status for the World Series was extremely doubtful.

What Staub was capable of accomplishing in the Fall Classic of 1973 was nothing short of extraordinary. Rusty was benched for the opener vs. Ken Holtzman, partially because he was left-handed but mostly because he was trying to convalesce his wounded shoulder. Staub actually was called upon to pinch hit against Rollie Fingers in the 9th, but Oakland A's skipper Dick Williams immediately brought in lefty Darold Knowles, effectively challenging Mets' manager Yogi Berra to make a countermove. Many observers felt Berra should have let Staub bat instead of immediately replacing him with a right-handed hitter. Yogi's "chess move" went for naught and the Mets lost, 2-1. Not wanting to go back to Shea down 0-2 and also not wanting to be further second-guessed, Berra started Staub in rightfield, even though Oakland was pitching another southpaw, Vida Blue. Rusty went 1-for-5, before being removed in a double switch, which resulted in Willie Mays' both embarrassing and redeeming himself, all within the span of a few minutes. Mays misplayed a fly ball off the wall, which ultimately allowed Oakland to tie the score and send the game into extra innings. Nevertheless, Willie made up for his miscue by sparking a 4-run rally with an RBI single and the Mets held on, 10-7.

Staub got two more hits in Game 3, playing with just a short-sleeved tee shirt under his uniform, despite the coldness of the New York night. Rusty never deviated from his normal routine and he wasn't about to start now, right shoulder separation notwithstanding. Mets' fans were rewarded for his diligence the next night, as he stole the show, socking a first inning three-run homer off Holtzman (who was ultimately knocked out of the box after retiring just one hitter), and then hitting a two-run single off Knowles, accounting for 5 RBI. One can only imagine what might have happened had Rusty been allowed to bat against Knowles in Game 1. Mets' fans can also further imagine how Staub might have fared with the function of *two* good arms. In the 7 games, he hit .423 with 11 hits (8 singles, 2 doubles, and 1 homer), 2 walks, 6 RBI and flawless fielding in the face of being forced to throw underhanded. One might have thought Staub and Milner could have been flip-flopped between rightfield and first base and given the Mets a sound outfield arm. Perhaps, the end result could have different and the Mets might have been World Champions instead of the A's, who repeated as "Kings of the Hill."

[Writer's note: I declared at the beginning that I would *not* critique on-the-field managerial decisions; I am merely speculating at other possible scenarios]. In fact, it was Yogi Berra, whose famous malapropism "It ain't over 'til it's over" was spawned by this improbable stretch, who made it possible for the Mets to be even be anywhere in a position to win a pennant, let alone a World Championship. When questioned about his strategies (such as not starting Stone at all, and letting both Seaver and Matlack pitch the last two games on three days rest in spite of going back to Oakland with a 3-2 lead in the Series), Berra employed a bit of "Stengelese" and replied, "Name me a team that ever went so much further than it was expected to go. I don't know baseball history *that* good to name one." As far as naming goes, Staub should definitely have been named the M.V.P. of the Series, regardless of the fact that he was on the losing side. His courageous performance ranks with some of the greatest in baseball legendry: i.e. Urban Shocker, who was suffering from heart disease but still on the roster as a pitcher, grooving pitches for the '27 Yankees during batting practice before the Series opener, supposedly helping intimidate the Pirates before the fact. Then there was the free-spirited journeyman righty (usually it's the lefties who are the goofy ones) Norman "Bobo" Newsom, who allegedly loved going to the racetrack even more than the ballpark. In 1940, he was a 21-game winner and helped pitch the Detroit Tigers to the A.L. pennant, breaking the Yankees' skein of four consecutive World Series titles. He won the opener in Cincinnati, 7-2, but that night found his beloved father dead of a heart attack in his hotel room. After his father's funeral two days later in South Carolina, Newsom rejoined the team and pitched a three-hit shutout at Detroit. On one day's rest, Newsom started and completed the 7th game, allowing only 2 runs and 7 hits, but the Tigers only pushed across one tally for him, and the Reds won their first untainted World Series Championship. Though Newsom would win a championship ring in '47 with the Yankees, it's this feat for which true baseball devotees'll always remember him, as well as for his off-the-field exploits.

Getting back to '73, there are many *other* devotees who dispute the validity of Reggie Jackson's winning the Series M.V.P. Award. Jackson deserved consideration, as did Bert Campaneris, Darold Knowles, and Ken Holtzman. Some sardonic aficionados even say Mike Andrews should be worthy of such praise: after all, it was his sudden dismal maltreatment by the dictatorial Athletics' owner Charlie Finley that made him the Jeanne d'Arc and *cause celebre* who united the "Fightin' A's." After making two critical errors that contributed to the A's loss in Game 2, Finley tried to have Andrews replaced in the middle of the Series with rookie Manny Trillo. The A's players threatened to boycott the rest of the Series and Baseball Commissioner Bowie Kuhn ordered Andrews' immediate reinstatement. Mike even got a standing ovation from the well-informed Shea Stadium crowd upon his introduction before Game 3. Nevertheless, the true M.V.P. was the gutsy Daniel Joseph "Rusty" Staub. Many "spoilt brats" of *his* era and today would have put their arms in a sling and collected splinters on the bench instead of producing on the field. Although Rusty would play a dozen more years in the big leagues, this was his only venture into the postseason, and he certainly made it a memorable one.

Staub had a decent season in 1974 even though the bottom dropped out on most of his teammates, as the Mets' finished 5th, 20 games under .500. In '75, Staub had his best season as a Met, with 19 homers, 30 doubles, 93 runs, 77 walks, a .282 batting average, a .448 slugging percentage, and an all-time team record of 105 RBI! He was named to the All-Star team (one of a handful to be so honored with 3 different squads) and was finally voted 1st team all-National League as an outfielder. Unfortunately, he fell prey to "The Grim Reaper of Grant's Tomb" and was traded in December to Detroit for Mickey Lolich. This time, the Mets' management *did* "pull an Otis," as Lolich was 35 and well past his glory days as a dominating left-handed pitcher, while Staub was consistently productive, highly popular with the fans and *almost* the entire organization, and at 3½ years Lolich's junior, still very much in his prime. "The Chairman of the Bored" may have been taking proactive measures in the event the players won their arbitration grievance and won the right to have open veteran free agency.

In any case, very much like the way Seaver was mistreated, it would take nearly half a decade to right this wrong, when the Mets were finally under new sounder ownership. But would it be too late? Would "The Curse of LeGrand Orange" go for the "hat trick?" Only time would tell and only sensible leadership could undo it.

#8 Combined High & Low Quality Move—Deroulet is De Ruler

It would be difficult, if not impossible, to call any of the moves made by the Mets' front office in the late 1970's "high quality." Most trades or free agent signings had disastrous results; the few that turned out all right had very extended delays before any kind of fruition was seen. For instance, when Jerry Koosman was traded to his native Minnesota after the 1978 season, the transaction yielded a young flame-throwing lefty who would be the Mets' ace reliever during the mid '80's: Jesse Orosco.

At the time, though, trading one of the few remaining links to their majestic era (although he was a combined 11-35 between 1977–1978) proved to be the last straw as far as Linda DeRoulet was concerned with M. Donald Grant's mishandling of her mother's franchise. The daughter of the late Mrs. Joan W. Payson fired Grant, but it was, as many aficionados observed, akin to "closing the barn door after the horses have all run out." At least it no longer allowed Grant to further play Hare Kari with the organization. Instead of entrusting any secondary club official to take over the operations, she took it upon herself to run the day-to-day business, despite her total lack of baseball knowledge (which, as has also been observed, never stopped any other owner). She had to take over an organization that had been systematically gutted for several years, fielded a lackluster major league squad, had few genuine minor league prospects, and was seriously dragging in the audience department. DeRoulet did hold over manager Joe Torre, who was popular with both the fans and players, and did the best he could with what he had.

Regrettably, the best Torre had to work with netted three consecutive last place finishes and equally abysmal attendance between 1977–1979. During that span, the Mets traded away (some of whom had been previously noted) Tom Seaver, Bud Harrelson, Jerry Grote, John Milner, Jon Matlack, and Jerry Koosman, who were part of the backbone of their contending years. Previously, Grant had whetted his scythe on the likes of (in succession) Tommie Agee, Jim McAndrew, Buzz Capra, Ray Sadecki, Duffy Dyer, Ken Boswell, Tug McGraw, Don Hahn, Teddy Martinez, Cleon Jones, Harry Parker, Wayne Garrett and Rusty Staub, each of whom had contributed to one or both of the Mets' pennant winning seasons. The team, in some instances, actually got some serviceable talent in return. Among some of the better players the Mets received were John Stearns, Mike Vail, Willie Montanez, Richie Hebner, Frank Taveras (trading Tim Foli whom they had reacquired off the waiver list in '77), and Skip Lockwood. The farm system in point of fact did occasionally develop (and hold onto) some decent prospects in those lean years (again, some of whom were already noted in this text): Craig Swan, William "Mookie" Wilson, Hubie Brooks, Wally Backman, Ron Gardenhire, Charlie Puleo, Jeff Reardon, Neil Allen, Alex Trevino, Nino Espinosa, and Brian Giles (no, not *that* Brian Giles; he was still only in 2nd grade, although he probably would have been able to outplay a lot of the guys the Mets had during this miserable period).

To use an expression earlier employed in the text, "Luck is the residue of design," and since the Mets were in such poor design, they wound up with more residue than luck. Swan, Stearns, Vail, Lockwood, and Gardenhire all were sufferers of career-shortening injuries. Puleo, Trevino, Espinosa, and Giles gave it their best efforts but never really panned out as "franchise" players that a contending team could be built around. As for Montanez, Hebner, and Taveras, they quickly wore out their welcome, as the Shea Stadium "boo-birds" had no patience for what they considered overpaid burned-out veterans with deteriorating skills and attitudes. The Mets had two potential righty closers in Allen and Reardon and for the time being, alternated them when given the opportunity. Of all the players developed, two of the most popular and gifted proved to be Wilson and Brooks, and the Mets publicity department did their best to promote them as the team's new "cornerstones." It would, however, require what was previously unthinkable in order to restore the Mets to their proper prominence: selling the entire organization.

DeRoulet continued in her role as director of operations, even while bids were being made to purchase the club. She actually pulled off what could have potentially been one of the best deals the Mets ever made: pitcher Craig Swan was traded to the California Angels for shortstop Dickie Thon and first baseman Willie Aikens. However, DeRoulet showed her complete naiveté in not only the sports industry but also the business world by voiding the deal because she was already in contract to sell the team.

In an age where in virtually all negotiations ulterior motives and underhanded tactics abound, DeRoulet's honesty and integrity were indeed refreshing.

#9 High Quality Move—New Ownership, At Last

Again, as previously stated with poetic license, "To err is human, to forgive is to be a Met fan." Met fans eventually forgave DeRoulet for any "transgressions" since she had sold the team to the partnership of Nelson Doubleday and Fred Wilpon, two men who had histories of sports involvement. Doubleday was a descendant of Colonel Abner Doubleday, who is given credit, as the legend goes, for creating the original incarnation of baseball back in 1839. This supposedly happened in the Upstate New York berg of Cooperstown, which until that time, was more famous for its namesake, author James Fenimore Cooper. Nearby Lake Otsego later became a summer resort, and then in 1939, during the alleged centennial of the sport's invention, Cooperstown is where the Baseball Hall-of-Fame was dedicated and has remained ever since.

Wilpon was the lesser known of the two men, but had been Sandy Koufax's friend and teammate while growing up in Brooklyn. Both Doubleday and Wilpon were learned businessmen and were smart enough to hire Frank Cashen, who had done such a marvelous job building the Baltimore Orioles organization in the 1970's, to take over as general manager. He was given a free hand in operating the club and the vast majority of his decisions paid off handsomely. Cashen brought over many people who had originally come from within the Orioles' system, including Joe McIlvane to be in charge of player development, George Bamberger as a special pitching instructor (who would take over as manager within a year), and Davy Johnson, who would "cut his own managerial teeth" in the Texas League with the Jackson AA Mets. Bamberger "fetched" his own set of coaches, including "The Capital Punisher," hitting instructor Frank Howard, who would, in 1983, step in temporarily as interim manager. Cashen knew that although he had "deep pockets" from which he could spend, the best choice was to build from within, through the draft and the farm system. The Mets had the first pick in the '80 amateur draft and picked Darryl Strawberry, while other players already in their organization were given their chance to exhibit their talent. This was done not just because the younger players were "hungrier," but to see what their trade value might be. As simple as it might sound, this is the *only* way to build a team! Cashen, although ridiculed at first by a hostile New York press corps, eventually "won them over" with his "wheeling-dealing."

#10 High Quality Move—Rusty's Return

Cashen also knew that, as his predecessors from the original Mets' front office discovered, you needed "nostalgia." Thus, in December 1980, nearly five years to the day he'd been exiled to the Motor City, Rusty Staub was signed as a free agent. He was slated to be a part time "1B/OF," as well as a pinch-hitter. This delighted Mets fans to no end, not only getting a quality veteran from their glory years, but the breaking of "The Curse of LeGrand Orange." While all the Mets' ills between 1976–1980 can't be blamed on Staub's absence, it certainly made at least superstitious fans feel better. The Expos had temporarily seen the light in when on the decade anniversary of the Apollo 11 moon landing (which seems to be an auspicious date in Staub's life), he was picked up after being released by the Tigers, and played a major role in their fight for the N.L. East title. The Pittsburgh Pirates won the division title on the last day of the regular season, and went on to triumph in their "We are Family" Championship of '79.

Rusty had had three solid seasons playing for manager Ralph Houk in Detroit, making the All-Star team all 3 years and being selected all-A.L. twice: once as an outfielder and once as a designated hitter. Missing only 4 games over the "trifecta," Rusty tallied 524 safeties (including 160 extra-base hits), 318 RBI, 232 runs, a .283 batting average and a .439 slugging percentage, both career norms. This time, though, Staub may have been a victim of his own alleged affliction as the Tigers' new manager was Sparky Anderson, a man Rusty grew to hate as much as he loved Ralph Houk. Anderson, who'd been fired after 9 extremely successful years with Cincinnati, did not acclimate well to his new environs and did several strange things, such as ordering the Tiger Stadium infield to be left to grow long. What that did make it nearly impossible for a ground ball to bounce through to the outfield and, for an admitted "plodder" like Staub, it was disastrous. Staub was placed on the disqualified list for a month for refusing to play at home under such ridiculous conditions. When he was finally reinstated (at the behest of the MLBPA), the situation remained intolerable and it was reflected in Rusty's lack of production (a .236 batting average, with 9 homers & 40 RBI in

68 games) until he finally returned to Montreal on July 20th. Incredibly, the Expos foolishly tempted fate and traded Staub to the Texas Rangers just before the start of the next season. Montreal could have possibly used his veteran leadership as they again battled for the division, this time losing out to Philadelphia the *next-to-last* day of the season. The Expos made it all the way to the NLCS in '81 (being one of the beneficiaries of the "split-season" set-up), had a two-games-to-one lead, but lost consecutive home games to the Los Angeles Dodgers, the last one on a 2-out homer in the 9th inning by Rick Monday. To many Expos' fans, the curse had reared its ugly head again and has never gone away.

There actually was no regular position for Staub on the Mets by 1981 (first base was occupied by Dave Kingman and then was later taken over in a standout manner by Keith Hernandez, they had a fairly solid outfield corps, and there was no designated hitter in the N.L.), but Rusty found work filling in when needed and being a spectacular pinch-hitter. In 1984, he tied 2 pinch-hitting records: he had 8 straight pinch-hits in 8 consecutive appearances, and totaled 24 off-the-bench in-the-clutch accomplishments.

He again played a key role in steadying the younger core of talent the Mets' management had augmented around him and the Mets won 188 games between '84 & '85, the most in the majors. Unfortunately, they came in second in the N.L. East both times (long before the advent of the "wild card"), but they drew huge crowds both at home and on the road, and played some exciting meaningful games for the first time in quite a while.

Fate was to play a cruel joke on Rusty and the Mets, mostly due to an agreement the MLBPA had reached in the two-day strike in August '85. All teams would attempt, on a temporary trial basis, to go with a *24*-man major league roster, including N.L. teams. This meant that players like Rusty and his genre (aging but still productive veterans who made solid contributions) could no longer be "carried" by the team. Thus, Rusty just missed out on being part of one of the dominant squads in history: the '86 Mets. They were the model of consistency (54-27 both at home and on the road) for a 108-54 record and a .667 winning percentage. They had no 20-game winner (5 won 14 or more, and 3 tallied 180 or more strikeouts). Catcher Gary Carter tied Staub's '75 record with 105 RBI, and the Mets persevered despite adversities. In mid-season, Rusty was honored at Shea, with several ex-teammates presenting gifts while lampooning him with orange fright wigs and stuffed uniforms. He'd have gladly traded it for a championship ring.

#9 Low Quality Move—First, The Bad News

When one is faced with the prospect of hearing both bad news and good news, simultaneously, very often one would rather hear the bad news first, so as to leave a more palatable "taste" to carry on with. Frank Cashen is arguably the best general manager (who also retained the roles as Executive Vice President and Chief Operating Officer) the Mets ever had. It's perhaps because as being empowered with this great authority that Cashen was able to accomplish so much with as little static as possible from the higher club echelons. The Mets had been burned before by people put in charge who turned to out to be megalomaniacs, or maniacs of a different kind. However, this time the ownership had chosen wisely and, in Frank Cashen, they had a man who was not afraid to make deals, but both never would alibi for a bad one or pat himself on the back too arduously when he made a good one. Luckily, the good ones far outweighed the bad.

His number one bad decision was to retain Joe Torre as manager. Torre had done a very respectable job with dreadful Mets teams in his 2½ years under the old regime. In fact, in 1976, he turned down a chance to be traded to the New York Yankees when they were on their way to winning a pennant in order to be in a position to manage the Mets the next season. He couldn't have taken it at the worse time, since the Mets' front office (spearheaded by You-Know-Who) was in the process of disassembling the entire organization, from top to bottom. Torre says he never regrets his decision, that it taught him to deal with adversity and gave him the chance to develop his managerial skills, literally from the ground up. He was also no stranger to disappointment, having never played in a post-season in 18 years and 2,200 games as a player, despite being the N.L. M.V.P. in 1971. He would get his first taste of playoff competition in 1982 as skipper of the Atlanta Braves, but that was short-lived as they were swept by, ironically enough, the St. Louis Cardinals, with whom he'd won his M.V.P. Another irony would arise when, finally, in 1996, two decades after declining an opportunity to play in the World Series with them, he would lead the Yankees to their first World title in 18 years and began a skein that was on a par with the Yankees' teams from 1936–39 and 1949–53.

Perhaps Cashen didn't want to appear callous by instantly firing Torre, but that was what ultimately happened before the end of the '81 season. Nice guys *do* finish last.

#10 Low Quality Move—More of the Bad News

When you're given little to work with, it's difficult to expect to get too much in return. Cashen was given relatively little talent with which to build on (compared to other franchises and Mets organizations of the past). Thus Cashen went about trying to get the right mix of players to make the Mets both exciting and competitive. One of the first deals he made was actually a pretty good one, obtaining outfielder Claudell Washington from the Chicago White Sox for pitcher Jesse Anderson. Claudell, in half a year, hit 10 homers, drove in 42, stole 17 bases, hit .275 and played a solid rightfield. The only problem was that Washington was a free agent, and although the Mets had greater resources to sign higher priced players, most players were still "steering clear" of Shea Stadium. Washington wound up signing with Atlanta. Very few people were buying into the propaganda being spread by the Della Femina ad agency (who had signed the Mets as a client) that "The Magic is Back!" A new owner can't instantly change the fortunes of an organization that had been in ruinous disrepair for years. It takes patience, by both the club and the fans, to get things turned around the right direction.

One thing the Mets (in all their incarnations) have been big on is nostalgia. This regime proved that by not only regaining Rusty Staub, but also trading Steve Henderson to the Cubs to get back Dave Kingman. Kingman had hit 73 homers in his previous two full seasons with the Mets ('75–'76) and might have been their first home-run title winner in his second year had he not dislocated his left thumb diving for a fly ball. He was traded to San Diego the same night as Tom Seaver had been traded to Cincinnati (6/15/77), an evening many writers dubbed "The Wednesday Night Massacre." In one stroke, the Mets (again everyone knows the "Mad General" was behind it) had brusquely cast out their two most popular players, including their best pitcher and power hitter.

Kingman quite literally traversed the country and the majors that year. After a month-and-a-half with the Padres, the California Angels claimed him on waivers. He hardly had time to unpack his swimming trunks when the Yankees claimed him again and he played a key role in their stretch drive towards the A.L. East title, although Kingman was ineligible for postseason play. Thus, he set a record that probably will never be equaled: playing for 4 teams in both the N.L. and A.L. East & West in the same season. Kingman signed as a free agent with the Chicago Cubs and had a decent three-year stint: 94 homers (including a majors-leading 48 in '79), 251 RBI, 193 runs, and (for him) a respectable .278 batting average. Regrettably, as intimidating and powerful as Kingman was (listed at 6'6" and 210 solid muscular pounds), he was ill suited to wearing any leather, except perhaps as a jacket. Whether at first base, third base, or in the outfield, his size (which would have been ideal for basketball) made him seem awkward, and he wore out his welcome in the Windy City. So, naturally, he's sent to a National League club (where there's no DH) and of course, the Mets gladly take him, looking for anyone who can, as Reggie Jackson once eloquently put it, "put the meat in the seats." Power-wise, Kingman delivered as reliably as possible, hitting 59 homers in 1981–82, and finally becoming the first Met in league history to lead the NL in home runs. However, he also achieved the unsavory distinction of having the lowest batting average (.204) of any home run title winner in major league history. Kingman was placed at first base, where the Mets management felt he could do his least amount of harm defensively. Then, exactly six years after he was unceremoniously given the heave-ho, another blow was dealt to his ego (which was larger than his batting average or defensive skills). The Mets acquired Keith Hernandez, who had won the Gold Glove 5 straight times (the streak would ultimately reach eleven, a record for first-sackers), and the batting title in '79, as well as being selected co-M.V.P. for that season. This reduced Kingman's role to a part-time 1B-OF and pinch-hitter; while Rusty Staub had no delusions of grandeur and was able to accept this role, Kingman was not. He sulked the rest of the season and was not offered salary arbitration, which left him free to play out his option. Kingman was originally from Oregon and had come up through the San Francisco chain, so he chose the best place he thought of to exhibit his skills and play close to home: Oakland. This way, he could DH and not have to worry about looking foolish in the field. Kingman had a very good season for the A's in '84 (.268 BA, 35 HR, 118 RBI), but he would never come close to repeating those stats. He retired with 442 lifetime homers, more than a third of them as a member of the Mets. While it's problematical to say he was well-liked and productive, one thing can't be denied: Kingman was certainly a very colorful Met.

#11 Low Quality Move—My 'Unfunny' Valentine

Another of Branch Rickey's adages was that it's best to trade a player a year too early than too late. That way, even if he has a productive season for another team, you might get equal or greater than equal trade value for him. Obviously, the Montreal Expos weren't thinking that way with regard to outfielder Ellis Valentine. For three seasons (from 1977–79), the outfield tandem of Warren Cromartie, Andre Dawson, and Valentine had been among the most productive offensively and feared defensively in baseball. Word got around quickly that you don't try to take extra bases on "The Crow," "The Hawk," or especially on "Cupid." Those years they led all outfield trios in assists and were part of the guts of the Expos teams looking to finally be considered a contender in the N.L. East.

Offensively, Valentine had also established himself as a consistent force, with 71 homers, 234 RBI, 37 steals, 92 doubles, a .286 batting average, and a .482 slugging percentage over that 3-year period. He was still only 25 years old going into the 1980 season and the sky seemed to be the limit. Ellis was on his way to perhaps his best season (with the Expos in full contention as they had been the year before) when he was the casualty of a fateful beaning, which left him with a fractured jaw and being gun-shy at home plate when he returned to action 5 weeks later. He still batted .315 and drove in 67 runs, but his dominance as a hitter was gone, and it could have possibly cost Montreal the division title. One might have argued that Rusty Staub, who'd been traded before that season had started, could have substituted temporarily and given Valentine a proper chance to recover. Ironically, Staub and Valentine would be reunited as teammates again.

As previously mentioned, the Mets had simultaneously developed two right-handed closers within their organization: Neil Allen, who was the more colorful of the duo, and Jeff Reardon, who was very steady and was usually put into service as a set-up man. The injured Valentine became available and the Expos were asking for a right-handed reliever in return; they left it up to the Mets to choose which of their two top prospects to swap. On paper, Allen looked like the better bet to keep since he was three years younger, had 22 saves the year before, and had become popular with the fans. Reardon, meanwhile, had developed herniated lower-back disc troubles as well as severe allergies. This led to one of the few poor choices by G.M./"Exec Veep"/C.O.O. Cashen. Three days after Memorial Day, 1981, Cashen made a very *un*memorable trade as far as Mets fans were concerned: he exchanged Jeff Reardon and outfielder Dan Norman (one of the "Fruitless Four," as they were dubbed, who the Mets got for Tom Seaver) for the still shaky Ellis Valentine. Norman can tell his grandkids, as the saying goes, that he was involved in two of the worst trades the New York Mets ever made. "Cupid" tried his best but his aim was errant: he batted a composite .254 with 16 homers, and 84 RBI over two seasons before the Mets let him play out his option and head for sunnier climes. Reardon went on to have one of the best careers a relief pitcher ever had, compiling 367 saves, which as of this writing, ranks *fourth* all-time. Reardon was also a key member of three post-season teams: the '81 Expos, the '87 Minnesota Twins, and the '90 Boston Red Sox. Although he could not help the "flanking" teams on this list win the pennant, his 31 saves, plus 2 apiece in the ALCS and the World Series secured the first championship in the history of the Twins. He also became the first pitcher in baseball history to notch two 40-save seasons: in '85 with Montreal and in '88 with Minnesota. Although this feat has become almost commonplace with many "ace" closers such as Dennis Eckersley, Trevor Hoffman, Robb Nen, Troy Percival, and Mariano Rivera, Reardon was the original.

As for Allen, he saved 37 over the next two seasons ('81 & '82), but unbeknownst to many people outside of baseball, he developed a severe drinking problem. Major league baseball had not as yet taken the tribulations of alcoholism and drug abuse very seriously—in fact, these "vices" were simply considered a part of the game that required attention only under very serious instances. It would be ironic that both the New York Mets and St. Louis Cardinals should see fit to, in a way, swap troubles. When Allen lost his closer role to lefty Jesse Orosco, he naturally didn't take it well and began a bender that soon put him on Frank Cashen's unwanted list. Keith Hernandez had fallen into similar circumstances in St. Louis, and Cashen saw a potential crisis as an opportunity. Thus, on what was the trading deadline at the time, the Mets swapped Allen and fellow pitcher Rick Ownbey to the Cardinals for Hernandez. Keith was hardly thrilled going from "the penthouse to the outhouse," but the fans made him feel welcome, and he decided he would make the most of it. After all, he seemingly had nowhere to go but up.

#11 High Quality Move—Taking It to the 'Mex'

The St. Louis Cardinals had just come off winning their first World Series in a decade-and-a-half and were in serious contention of repeating as the spring of 1983 drew to a close. Their All-Star first baseman was a significant factor in their success and was only 29 years old and seemingly in good physical health. He was a solid .299 lifetime hitter coming into this season, and had absolutely no peer when it came to fielding his position. He had won 1 batting title and tied for a National League M.V.P. Award. His seven hits and eight RBI were crucial to the Cardinals' clinching their Championship. Given all this information, it would seem totally illogical for Cards' manager Dorrel (which rhymes with squirrel) "Whitey" Herzog to insist that Keith Hernandez be traded to *any* team, let alone the lowly New York Mets. When questioned about this, Herzog's reply was as ridiculous a reason as has ever been given for any such treatment of a player: Hernandez was too interested in doing his crossword puzzles in the clubhouse.

However, many of the real reasons Herzog had become disgusted with Hernandez did not fully come out for more than two years when new MLB Commissioner Peter Ueberroth called for widespread investigations of cocaine use by baseball players. According to his own testimony, Hernandez had been what he described as a "controlled" addict, using it only when he felt he needed a boost (as opposed to habitually or on a constant basis) and always in private (on the Pittsburgh Pirates, many players allegedly "did lines" en masse right off the trainer's table). Keith also claimed he had been "clean" long before his banishment from the organization he'd spent his entire career ever since graduating from high school. Herzog asserted that he had delayed taking such measures until he saw the situation getting out of hand with some of Hernandez's teammates, and "Mex" was branded the scapegoat. Hernandez originally was going to refuse to report to the Mets (he couldn't have refused the trade—he didn't qualify for the '10-and-5'), but was convinced by GM Frank Cashen that the team was in a rebuilding stage and that they wanted him to be one of the "pillars." Mets' fans are certainly glad he came aboard.

All Hernandez did over the next five years was hit .303 with 232 extra-base hits, score 428 runs with 420 RBI, win the Gold Glove for N.L. first basemen every year, finish 2nd in the M.V.P. voting in '84, and lead them to a World Championship in '86.

In 1988, Keith won his eleventh consecutive Gold Glove; he also started having serious injury problems for the first time in his career. He spent nearly two months on the disabled list due to hamstring pulls, and was limited to appearances in just 95 games, the first time in a dozen years he had played in less than a hundred contests, including the '81 strike season. "Mex" also had less than 100 hits for the first time since he was sent back to AAA ball his second year with the Cards. The Gold Glove and a .276 average (including 16 doubles and 11 homers) helped salvage part of the season, and his plucky performance in a losing effort in the NLCS (7 hits & 5 RBI) elicited images of one his predecessors at first: Rusty Staub. Unfortunately, the next year brought more of the same as he did another two-month stint on injured reserve.

If his initial trade to the Mets had shocked Hernandez, then the truly unthinkable happened: he was benched. Between his injuries and lack of productivity, manager Davy Johnson had to make the anguished decision to sit down a man who was one of the foundations of the team's resurgence during the 1980's. Hernandez hit only four more homers for the Mets and was not offered a contract for 1990. As the saying goes, "the brain admits what it takes the heart much longer to accept." In his heart, Hernandez believed he could still produce. He signed a minor league contract with the Cleveland Indians (who ironically were also in a serious rebuilding process, much the way the Mets were when they acquired Hernandez). "Mex" actually made it back to the majors, but his enthusiasm was short-lived and he had to retire soon after. His lifetime .296 BA, 1,124 runs, 2,182 hits, and 1,071 RBI over 12 seasons (plus portions of 5 others) are fairly impressive. Add into that 11 straight Gold Gloves and being a recognized leader of World Championships on two different squads could rate Hall-of-Fame consideration, if only on a borderline basis at best. Keith had the disastrous misfortune to get caught up in the morass of narcotics that all sports (both pro & amateur) seem to be ensnared in.

Nevertheless, Keith was still voted by the fans as the greatest first baseman in Mets' history for their 40th Anniversary celebration. He currently works as a color commentator for the team on its local broadcast T.V. airings. "Mex" is as unflinching as a broadcaster as he was charging almost straight into home plate on bunt plays.

#12 High Quality Move—"Ambi-Maz" for 2 Good Arms

The Mets' number one draft choice in the 1973 amateur draft was a handsome ambidextrous outfielder who looked like he could have stepped right off of central casting for "Happy Days," "Saturday Night Fever" or "The Karate Kid." He was a "five-tool" player, as the expression goes, and in Willie Mays' last year in the majors, he was already being touted as Mays' successor. To top it all off, he came from Brooklyn, which made him an automatic heartthrob to most of the female New York Mets' fans.

His name is Lee Louis Mazzilli, but quickly became known as Maz, almost as quickly as he ascended through the minors and made his Met debut at age 21. Being from the Big Apple, he didn't fall prey to the same syndrome that affected prospects such as Amos Otis and Nolan Ryan. He was able to handle the big city pressure, the extreme fickleness of the fans, and playing at Shea Stadium, which could hardly be called the most attractive home field. Even as the club was disintegrating around him, Maz lived up to his billing and became the team's most popular and productive player. In his first four full seasons, he batted .277, slugged .414, scored 304 runs, drove in 262, had 117 steals, and was named to three All-Star teams. He remained one of their few (if not their only) drawing card, even when the club came under new management in 1980.

However, even Maz was not immune to the unpleasant reality of losing his job to a younger, more talented player. Maz was not benched, simply moved to leftfield to make room for one of the "cornerstones" of the new regime: Mookie Wilson. When interviewed about the move, Maz made the inopportune statement that "it takes a genius to play centerfield, but any idiot can play leftfield." Of course, he was speaking out of anger and rejection, and although it didn't cost him his starting job, it also didn't win him any favor with the management, nor did it win him any friends among fellow leftfielders such as Dave Winfield, Gary Matthews, Jose Cruz, Dusty Baker, Tim Raines, Rickey Henderson, and still

"The King of Kings" as far as leftfielders were concerned, Carl Yastrzemski. What Maz was merely reacting to was what he perceived as the club tinkering in an area where he felt it needed no improvement. Had he expressed his feelings *that* way, it's doubtful there would have been any backlash from the fans or the organization at all. Further insult arose when Maz began platooning at first base. Thus, after Maz batted a career low .228 in 95 games of the strike-shortened '81 season, he was traded to the Texas Rangers for two of their best young budding pitchers: Ron Darling and Walt Terrell. Darling spent 2 seasons at Triple-A Tidewater, where despite showing good "stuff," he had a wildness problem (much the way Nolan Ryan did). The Mets liked what they saw in his September '83 call-up, posting a 2.80 ERA, allowing only 31 hits in $35^1/_3$ innings and striking out 27. When Davy Johnson took over the parent club in '84, he brought his hard-throwin' Hawaiian with him who very soon, was the Number 2 starter. Who became the No. 1 starter is a tragedian tale unto itself for later in this text.

Meanwhile, Charles Walter Terrell had been the winningest pitcher in the Texas League in '81, and while he didn't exactly tear up the International League with Tidewater (a 7-8 record, a 3.96 ERA, and only 74 strikeouts in 139 innings), he was actually promoted to the majors before Darling, losing all three of his starts at the end of '82. He was given more seasoning in '83 (with a 10-1 mark, leading the IL in winning percentage) and was brought up again at mid season to stay. Terrell was 8-8 with a 3.57 ERA, and had an excellent hits to innings ratio of 123 to $133^2/_3$ for an 8.28 average of safeties per nine-innings pitched. He was being counted on as a regular starter.

It's always nice if a trade works out well for all parties concerned, but the Mets have been burned so often in their history, it's difficult for any fans or anyone within their organization to feel badly when someone they exchanged (especially someone who had been so popular) doesn't fare particularly well. After not exactly lighting it up at Arlington Stadium, the Rangers traded Mazzilli to the Yankees even up for Bucky Dent. It's ironic that two such popular former New York All-Stars should eventually be traded for each other. Maz also didn't perform greatly in Yankee pinstripes, partially due to a fractured wrist, with which he insisted on playing. The Yanks rewarded his devotion by trading him over the winter to Pittsburgh for four minor leaguers, including Tim Burke, who would go on to later fame as a closer for the Montreal Expos.

Mazzilli was now gone from the Big Apple, but his commitment to relatively clean living would eventually give him a second chance with his original club, and he would assist them in ways he couldn't have ever possibly imagined.

#13 High Quality
Move—Summoning The Doctor

Perhaps once every generation comes a major league pitcher who can truly be called, as one writer put it, "The King of Smoke." In the teens & 20's, it was "The Big Train," Walter Johnson who far outpaced all others as far as strikeouts were concerned. His 21-year total of 3,508 was once thought to be among baseball's unbreakable records, and it did stand for 56 years until the "undisputed King of Smoke," Nolan Ryan, broke it. "Ryan's Express," in fact, "raised the bar" to an almost unreachable level of 5,714, as he spanned 4 different decades, also setting single season, and consecutive season marks.

In between these two "locomotives" several other hurlers with equally impressive "motors" made the grade as strikeout artists. "Rapid" Robert Feller, who fanned 15 in his first big-league start and followed that up three weeks later with a record-tying 17 K's, before he had even turned 18, looked like a good bet to challenge Johnson's lifetime standard. In his first six years, Feller had averaged 7.66 strikeouts-per-nine innings and already was about a third of the way to Johnson's paradigm, when at age 23, he enlisted in the Navy the day after the Pearl Harbor attack. Feller missed all of '42, '43, & '44 while aboard ship in the North Atlantic. He was given his honorable discharge after Germany surrendered and, even though the war was still going on vs. Japan, because he was the sole support of his family (Feller's father had died while Bob was out at sea), he was allowed to resume his previous means of living (and thereby collect his former salary) at once. Along with players like Hank Greenberg and Ted Williams, Feller was a true hero.

After getting his feet wet again in '45, Feller came back like gangbusters in '46 and had his best strikeout season with 348. He would pace the A.L. in K's the next two years, win 20 twice more, and lead the Indians to a championship in '48 and a pennant in '54, but Feller was never quite the same after losing those 3½ seasons to the war. His career total of 2,581 is still good enough for 21st on the all-time list, but it's possible Feller could have struck out around a thousand or so hitters during those years he missed and have been the first to surpass Johnson.

However, Feller never speaks bitterly about any missed opportunity. He'd be the first to say he "helped set by far the most important record of all: we won the war!" The only "beef" Feller has is with the Hall of Fame; he has led a campaign to get the Cooperstown brass to have the service records of all those enshrined put on their plaques, as opposed to there just being time gaps listed. As WWII veterans are dying every day, it would be a relatively simple request to comply with.

Any discussion about strikeouts would be delinquent without mentioning who, as the line from the film *On the Waterfront* goes, "could'a been a contenda:" Sanford Koufax. It's significant that a Brooklyn-esque brogue would be evoked when speaking of Koufax, since he both came from there and pitched for the professional baseball club that called there home. Koufax signed a bonus contract in 1955 after spending just one year at Cincinnati University on a combined baseball-basketball scholarship. At the time, there were no rules about signing college athletes in the midst of their matriculation, except that they lost their amateur status. However, MLB had developed a compromise before there was an official free agent draft. Any rookie who did not spend at least his first full year on the major league roster would be subject to a "first-year" player draft. The Dodgers had lost Roberto Clemente the year before in this manner and were determined it would not be repeated. Thus, Koufax, at 19 years old and having nowhere near the seasoning necessary to be successful, was nonetheless placed on the 25-man roster. He got into 12 games, started 5, and even pitched 2 shutouts, was wild, allowing 28 walks and 33 hits in $41^2/_3$ innings. Sandy sat on the bench as their 11th pitcher during the entire World Series, but may have been a good luck charm as the Dodgers finally beat the New York Yankees for their first (and only) championship in Brooklyn. Things didn't improve for Koufax the following year as in 16 games (10 of which were starts), he threw no complete games, his ERA ballooned to 4.91 and his base runners swelled to 95 in $58^2/_3$ innings. Again, Koufax didn't throw a pitch in what turned out to be the last Subway Series for 44 years, but this time the "Brooks" lost in 7 games.

For the next four years, even after the Dodgers moved operations to Los Angeles, Koufax continued to spin his wheels, but the club was reticent to send him down to the minors for fear that another team might draft him. After a half-dozen years, he was 4 games under .500, with personal bests of 11 victories (in '58), an ERA of 3.91, 7 CG's, 175 IP and 197 K's, all achieved in 1960. L.A. brass hoped the adage about lefties taking longer to develop was true. Then, in spring training of '61, he got the best advice yet. Second-string catcher Norm Sherry simply told Sandy that he doesn't have to throw each pitch so hard every single time. He got Koufax to slow down his mechanics and use his great physical gifts more, such as his long lean muscular arms and his great balance to create more of, as one commentator put it, a "bow-and-arrow" effect. The positive results were immediate as Koufax had a then-career high 18 victories, lowered his ERA to 3.52, had 15 CG's, and led the majors in strikeouts with 269 in $255^2/_3$ IP. This was merely a harbinger of incredible greatness, as Sandy led the N.L. in ERA in each of the next five years (including three times under 2.00), led in strikeouts thrice (his 382 total in '65 still standing as the N.L. record), in shut-outs 3 times (including eleven in his M.V.P. year of '63), and victories three times ('63, '65, & '66—which happened to be the years he won the Cy Young Award). Koufax was also M.V.P. of the World Series twice: in '63, when he set the southpaw record for strikeouts in a World Series game (15) vs. the Yankees, and in '65, when he pitched two complete game shutouts in a four-day span vs. the Twins. The Dodgers won the Series both times, as well as in '59 when he lost Game 5 vs. the Chicago White Sox at the L.A. Coliseum in front of the largest crowd in Series' history: 92,706. Sandy pitched 7 innings and gave up only 1 run (on a double play grounder) but still lost. The Dodgers won the pennant half the years Sandy was with them.

Koufax would pitch one more season ('66), and make it one for the books: 27-9, a 1.73 ERA, 27 CG's, 41 starts, 323 innings, 317 strikeouts, and 5 shutouts, all of which stats led the N.L. and all were necessary for the Dodgers to beat out the San Francisco Giants by 1½ games. Then in the World Series, he was victim-ized by centerfielder Willie Davis' three errors on two consecutive plays in Game 2, and was removed after giving up only 2 earned runs in 6 innings. Two months later, Koufax officially called it a career at age 30, owing to continuous awful pain in his left elbow and not wanting to chance having his arm amputated. The place his total of 2,396 K's puts him on the all-time list matches his uniform number, 32, and he averaged better than a K-an-inning, having pitched $2,324^1/_3$ IP for his career. He's one we as fans are left to ponder, "What if?"

The ultimate "What if?" query about strikeout records, though, has to be reserved for the man who was the Mets' # 1 pick in the 1982 amateur draft (and #2 overall behind shortstop Shawon Dunston): Dwight Gooden. He was drafted right out of high school in Tampa, Florida, and immediately posted "Koufax-like" numbers. In his two minor league seasons, he was 24-9 with a composite 2.57 ERA in $269^2/_3$ innings and a startling 384 strikeouts. There were officials within the Mets organization who did *not* want to promote Gooden to the big leagues, feeling he was still only 19 and could use at least one season at the Triple-A level. Luckily, Davy Johnson was taking over as Mets' manager and became

Gooden's strongest advocate *against* keeping him at Triple-A. He only needed to cite a recent example of how not properly promoting a player (especially when he greatly outdistanced the competition) could be harmful. The year before, Darryl Strawberry was by far the best outfielder in the Mets' camp, but in an effort not to rush him or make it seem they were desperate, the Mets brass sent him to Triple-A. After just 16 games, he finally made the jump to the big leagues, but his progress was temporarily retarded by not starting with the parent club from the beginning of the season. Darryl eventually straightened himself out and his 26 homers and 19 steals earned him N.L. Rookie-of-the-Year honors. Nevertheless, it taught the Mets a bitter lesson.

Mostly at Johnson's behest, Gooden was included on the major league roster and in the starting rotation, ultimately working his way into being the Number 1 starter. His rookie season is the kind most ballplayers can only dream of. He was 17-9, was second in the majors in ERA at 2.60 (and had the best among any pitchers with 200 or more innings), and led the majors with a rookie-record shattering 276 K's, a record formerly held by Hall-of-Famer Grover Cleveland Alexander and had stood for 73 years! He also broke the record for strikeouts-per-9 innings in a season with 11.4. Gooden was one of the main reasons for the 2nd best one-year turnaround in Mets history: in 1969, they had improved 27 victories and won the World Series; this year, they advanced 22 games and went from dead last to second in the N.L. East. Gooden was a unanimous choice for N.L. Rookie-of-the-Year, was selected 1st team all-N.L. (despite Chicago's Rick Sutcliffe winning the Cy Young Award for $2/3$ of a season's work), and earned some M.V.P. votes.

If Gooden was worried about a sophomore jinx, he sure didn't show it and he sure didn't take any prisoners in '85. He won the ERA title with an astounding 1.53 grade, the lowest in baseball since Bob Gibson's astonishing record 1.12 in 1968, under the old "Year of the Pitcher" conditions. Gooden also finished with a 24-4 record, the first time since 1963, when Sandy Koufax was 25-5, that any N.L. pitcher was 20 or more games over .500. As a note of interest, both Gibson and Koufax were voted M.V.P. of the National League in those respective seasons. It helped that both of their teams won the pennant; it certainly wasn't Gooden's fault that despite securing 98 victories, the Mets were unable to win the N.L. East, as the St. Louis Cardinals won three more. Moreover, Gooden won the pitching "Triple Crown" by leading the league in wins, ERA, and K's (268). It was all those K's that earned Dwight the nickname of "Doctor K," as a parody on Julius Erving's handle, "Doctor J." Fervent Met fans started the "K-Corner," where they would tally up Gooden's strikeouts with giant "K" placards taped to the façade of the upper deck at Shea. This soon caught on at other stadia but originated in New York.

Had Gooden sustained this kind of productivity for the entire length of his career, there's no telling what kind of statistics he could have compiled. He'd already won N.L. ROTY, been selected unanimous N.L. Cy Young Award winner (finishing fourth in the M.V.P. voting), and was about to be involved in one of the most dominating seasons any team has ever accomplished. The '86 Mets, as has been previously mentioned, pounded out 108 victories and won the N.L. East by 20 games over their nearest competitor, the Philadelphia Phillies. They didn't have any individual title winner, but collectively they led baseball in hitting and pitching. They carried a swagger, almost an arrogance, which rubbed many other teams the wrong way. Three different brawls "lowlighted" their otherwise astronomically superlative season. The two that were *on* the field both involved third baseman Ray Knight, a former Golden Gloves boxer (who is also married to pro lady golfer Nancy Lopez) and a personal reclamation project of manager Johnson. It was Johnson who insisted on acquiring Knight from Houston two years earlier and stuck with him when right elbow problems hampered both his hitting and fielding. A successful operation in the off-season had Knight flashing shades of his former self. In late May, the Mets faced the Dodgers at Shea Stadium in what many thought would be a prelude to the NLCS. The two teams had had a brawl the year before in which one of the Mets' pitchers, Ed Lynch, was seriously injured and may have cost them a shot at the division title (few Mets fans shed any tears when Dodgers' outfielder Pedro Guerrero—who was deeply involved in that fracas—tore up his knee at the start of the season). There was a natural inborn rivalry between the two teams, especially when playing in New York, and the "boo-birds" at Shea were really letting L.A. relief pitcher Tom Niedenfuer have it, constantly reminding him of the 2 home runs he surrendered in *last* year's playoffs, both of which ultimately cost his team the pennant. When his "rabbit ears" could not tune out the distractions, he finally took his frustration out on Knight, nailing him in the back with a fastball. Knight, without any hesitation, charged the mound, grabbed the much bigger Niedenfuer (who was 3 inches taller and 45 pounds heavier) around the waist, wrestled him to the ground just off the pitcher's mound and pounded away at his back. Knight was ejected but it set the tone for a season in which the Mets would establish themselves as a team to be reckoned with and not messed with.

The other brawl involving Knight took place at Cincinnati and featured a new "heavyweight contender:" utility man Kevin Mitchell. After Knight and Cincinnati outfielder Eric Davis had collided in a play at third base, Davis put both his forearms into Knight's chest and Knight instantly put a right cross into Davis' jaw. Both benches and bullpens cleared (reminiscent of the skirmish in the '73 playoffs), and the most vivid image is that of Kevin Mitchell being surrounded like a bear fighting off a pack of wolves. Over a half-dozen Reds must have tried their hand at Mitchell only to get much more of their anatomy crushed in return. 4 Met regulars were ejected, leaving the Mets with only seven position players. Manager Johnson was forced to "earn his salary" that night, as he alternated his righty-lefty relief tandem of Roger McDowell and Jesse Orosco between the mound and rightfield. The strategy worked beautifully, and they were even allowed 8 warm-up pitches each time they came back to pitch. The Mets were vindicated when Howard Johnson (who was playing shortstop, while Gary Carter played third, and backup catcher Ed Hearn was behind the plate) hit a 3-run homer in the 12th inning.

The *off*-the-field scuffle happened outside a bar in Houston, right before the All-Star Break. Three Mets pitchers (Gooden not being one of them—he would have his own brushes with the law, soon enough) had taken second baseman Tim Teufel out for a celebration of his "new arrival from the stork." However, Houston police swooped down more like vultures when Teufel walked outside the bar with his alcoholic beverage still in his hand. Teufel's teammates sprung to his defense and the result was perhaps the most overzealous Texas police response since the Vietnam War protests. All four Mets wound up under arrest and spent the night in jail. The New York tabloids made light of the incident (one "rag" featuring the headline "The Boys of Slammer"), but to those involved and under indictment for drunk and disorderly behavior, it was no laughing matter. Everyone involved had to return after the season to face charges, but each was ultimately just given probation and a fine. It was a microcosm of the end of an era, when athletes' offenses against humanity, whether real or contrived, would neither be tolerated nor covered up by the media. Conversely, the press looked for any kind of dirt it could find.

Gooden, meanwhile, had a decent season, but nothing like his previous two super overpowering campaigns. He went 17-6 with a 2.84 ERA and struck out exactly 200, becoming the first pitcher in baseball history to record 200 or more strikeouts his first three full seasons. Gooden also pitched very well in the NLCS, allowing only 2 runs in 17 innings, but only having a loss and no decision to show for it. Luckily, the Mets were able to pull out one of the most exciting playoff series ever, winning 3 games in their last at bat. In the World Series, though, "Doc" was at his worst, surrendering 8 runs in 9 IP and deservedly getting tagged with 2 losses. Again, the Mets were almost providential, as twice they were one strike away from losing the Series in Game 6, only to be rescued by both their own intestinal fortitude and, some say, "The Curse of the Bambino." They similarly came back in Game 7 (although not in so nearly dramatic fashion), beat the Red Sox, and won their 2nd World Championship.

With the young pitching staff they had possession of, and other position players poised to have good careers, the Mets should have been able to continue their domination of baseball. "Doc" would wind up being the poster boy for Mets' underachievement.

#12 Low Quality
Move—Adopting a Foster Adult

The old regime, despite making many good trades (until the "Emperor's" Kamikaze act perpetrated during the late 1970's) had a penchant for obtaining players who were well past their prime. All teams do this from time to time, because often a trade or a free agent signing is literally a crapshoot: you don't know exactly what you're going to get from a player. When the Mets attained George Foster from Cincinnati a few weeks before spring training 1982, however, it seemed as if they had finally "landed a good one." He was only 33 years old, in good shape, and had an incredibly productive year in '81 considering he was only able to participate in 108 games due to the players strike: 22 homers, 90 RBI, a .295 batting average and .519 slugging percentage in helping lead the Reds to the best overall record in baseball. However, because of the stupidity of the "split-season" structure, Cincinnati was left completely in the cold. Partially due to the bitterness caused by this injustice, and, as previously mentioned about Tom Seaver's reacquisition, Reds' management was looking to unload huge salaries and, in doing so, dismantling the "The Big Red Machine." Tony Perez, Rawly Eastwick, Pete Rose, Joe Morgan, Ken Griffey, Don Gullett, Ray Knight and others who had been members of their division winning teams were summarily let go or replaced with other, less-costly players, without regard to the team's performance or fans' reaction.

Despite leading the league in RBI three straight years, setting a one-season team record with 52 homers, winning the 1977 N.L. M.V.P. Award and contributing mightily to their back-to-back championships in '75–'76, Foster's turn to be cast aside finally came, and all the Mets gave up for him was a backup catcher and two relief pitchers. He was the sort of front-line talent the Mets had been seeking five years earlier when they traded Seaver. The new administration of Doubleday, Wilpon, and Cashen truly believed they had partly righted that wrong. However, things would not pan out as planned.

Perhaps it was the pressure of signing a lucrative long-term contract, or trying too hard to justify the fans' and management's expectations, but George had his most miserable full season, hitting only .247 with 13 HR & 70 RBI and was a constant target of criticism, both at the ballpark and in the media. The next year, his power numbers improved (28 HR & 90 RBI), but his hitting worsened and the Mets finished last, again. By 1984, more help had arrived and George had a decent season (.269/24/86) as the Mets enjoyed a revival they hadn't experienced in a decade-and-a-half. As previously listed in this text, the Mets jumped from last to 2nd place, with Dwight Gooden, Ron Darling, Jesse Orosco, Keith Hernandez, and Darryl Strawberry putting together fine seasons, and Foster, among others, doing *their* parts. This silver cloud had one dark lining: Foster had to be removed from the cleanup spot. Even though Foster outhit Strawberry by 18 points, George couldn't match his 26 homers and 97 RBI, and manager Johnson figured Foster could "protect" Darryl in the line-up better, especially when facing lefties. Outwardly, Foster never complained but one had to know it was a blow to his ego. It didn't help his image with the fans when he refused to take a curtain call for hitting his 300th homer.

The following year, his ego took another ambush when the Mets obtained Gary Carter from Montreal, and Foster would now be batting *sixth* instead of *fifth*. His "power supply" dwindled even further to 21 HR & 75 RBI as the Mets battled down to the wire for the N.L. East title against the St. Louis Cardinals. In the last game between the two teams, when a Met win would have pulled them into a tie for first place, all of Foster's frustrations and disappointments were summed up in one at bat. With the bases loaded and one out, Foster had a golden opportunity to be a hero and break the game open. Instead, he failed as a Met where he had succeeded so many times as a Red, hitting a meek ground ball that went for a force out at home. There was no further scoring in the inning and the Mets lost by one run. Some writers and fans blamed Foster's seeming lack of caring. No one can really tell what's in one's mind, but Foster had taken his own failure apparently too much in stride, for many people's liking.

He was still the regular leftfielder the next year, when the Mets ran away with the division. The team was willing to tolerate his relative lack of productivity (only 13 HR & 37 RBI) by August, but *not* his unwarranted racist public comments about club policy regarding the development of young prospects. He was released (and paid off the remainder of his contract in one lump sum) and ironically replaced by one of the finest prospects the team ever produced, Lee Mazzilli. Under different circumstances, Foster's career #'s of 347 HR & 1,232 RBI might warrant HOF consideration. It's now doubtful.

#14 High Quality Move—HoJo, The Kid & Sid

When playing chess, a good player needs to think several moves ahead as he or she devises a strategy. The Mets had improved 32% victory-wise from 1983 to 1984 and had contended for the division title until the last week of the season (ironically, the Cubs clinched on September 24th, 15 years to the day after the Mets had clinched the National League Eastern Division over them).

Many general managers would have stood pat and sat on their laurels, but not Frank Cashen. He turned two off-season deals that proved extremely critical to the Mets' success for years to come. First, on December 6, 1984, he traded pitcher Walt Terrell even up to Detroit for infielder Howard Johnson. He had hit 12 homers and driven in 50 runs in part-time play, but similar to Rusty Staub, had fallen out of favor with Tigers' manager Sparky Anderson. Johnson was limited to one pinch-hitting appearance in the ALCS and was completely frozen out of the World Series. Anderson preferred to use back-up catcher Manny Castillo as his third baseman in the five-game triumph over the San Diego Padres. The Tigers may have overcome "The Curse of LeGrand Orange," which still afflicts the Astros and the Expos, but since then they've been plagued with the dreaded "HoJo Hex." Detroit has not won the pennant since '84, and even Anderson admitted, years later, that it was the worst case of personnel assessment of his career.

Johnson would go on to be a key member of the Mets' '85 contending team and their '86 Championship team, before taking over full time at third base in '87. HoJo became the only third baseman to join the "30-30" club three times ('87, '89, '91). In '91, he was the first Met in history to lead the N.L. in home runs & RBI (38 & 117, respectively). When Jeff Torborg took over as manager in '92, the first "bright" move he made was to try to turn the "30-30 3B" into an outfielder. This idiotic gesture, along with Johnson's becoming a Born-Again Christian (which has been documented as often diminishing a player's desire to excel), caused his career to plummet and ultimately end within 2 years. However, HoJo was still voted by the fans as the best "hot corner" man in team history, thereby breaking a so-called jinx on the position (a well-known piece of lore among Mets' fans—they had averaged better than 4 third basemen per season) and establishing a hex on the team he originally signed with but had given up on him.

When this trade was consummated, it left the Mets with the dilemma of having 2 third basemen (3, if you counted the injured Ray Knight). Both Hubie Brooks and Johnson could cover shortstop admirably, but would have ultimately gotten in each other's way. Mr. Cashen solved this potential problem four days later, when he pulled off a blockbuster, sending Brooks, catcher Mike Fitzgerald, outfielder Herm Winningham and pitcher Floyd Youmans to Montreal for All-Star backstop Gary Carter. Carter had been named 1st-team All-N.L. 3 of the last 4 years, and 2nd-team All-N.L. 4 times in his 9 full seasons with the Expos, after originally breaking in as an outfielder. He had tied for the league lead in RBI with 106 and was in the midst of doing a "rubber-chicken" publicity tour for the Expos. However, between his "Apple Pie" image rubbing both his teammates and the organization the wrong way, and his needing surgery to repair knee cartilage damage, Montreal saw a chance to rid itself of what it considered an overpriced egocentric headache. This probably hurt Carter far worse than any pain in his knees.

In any case, the surgery was successful and his ego was buoyed by the welcome he was given both by the fans and by his new mates. He rewarded them by hitting .281, socking 32 homers and driving in 100, while steadying the young Met pitching staff and leading them to the brink of the N.L. East title (which 98 wins would have secured in just about any other season). It was more of the same next year, as Carter's 105 RBI (despite missing 3 weeks with a dislocated thumb) tied Rusty Staub's 1975 team record. More importantly, Gary led the Mets all the way the championship. In spite of a dreadful slump, he drove in the winning run in NLCS Game 5. He then smacked 2 homers over the "Green Monster" as the Mets tied the World Series vs. Boston at 2 games apiece. Then, in Game 6, with the Mets 2 runs down and one out away from elimination, Gary ignited the rally that enabled the Mets to pull out a miraculous (there's *that* word again) 6-5 victory. They would overcome a 3-run 6th inning deficit in Game 7 and Carter would finally have his well-earned championship. No one in the "Big Apple" was complaining about his "Apple Pie" except perhaps viewers of an ill-conceived team video, in which the theme was "Let's Go, Mets," and Carter and Hernandez were the main cheerleaders.

Unfortunately, age, injury, and the grind of 11 years of squatting behind home plate took its toll on "The Kid." His production sank to 20 HR & 83 RBI in '87 and to 11 HR & 46 RBI in '88, although he did manage to hit his 300th career homer and lead the Mets to the division title. His abysmal performance in the NLCS (6 for 27) was partially responsible for the Mets being upset by the L.A. Dodgers in seven games. In '89, Carter hit rock bottom, spending 2½ months on the disabled list, and, coincidentally, both he and Keith Hernandez were benched and subsequently not tendered contracts for 1990. Carter played with the Giants in '90, the Dodgers in '91, and finally he returned home triumphantly to Montreal in '92 before calling it a career. The Expos' hat is what he chose to have bronzed on his Hall-of-Fame plaque, although he won his championship with the Mets. Carter claims the Hall-of-Fame chose the logo; we can ponder how he really feels. In any case, the Mets' fans can take pride in "The Kid" just the same.

A relatively unheralded transaction took place the year before these two far more publicized ones. The Mets and Dodgers swapped young hard-throwing southpaws and utility men for each other on December 8, 1983. Bob Bailor and Carlos Diaz, who had pitched fairly well for the Mets in relief and spot-starting, were sent to L.A. for Ross Jones and a rotund Hawaiian (as opposed to Ron Darling, who was svelte) named Charles Sidney Fernandez. Fernandez exhibited good stuff in '84 spring training, but was a bit wild (as young hard-throwing southpaws tend to be) and he was the last pitcher cut from the opening day roster. Also, manager Johnson felt that Fernandez could do with work on his control, with both his pitches and his silverware. Sid was eventually able to get his fastball and curve under wraps, plus developing a "slide step" to keep baserunners from getting too big a lead and stealing at will. However, despite many diets and several times going up and down with his weight, Fernandez usually tipped the scales at a reported 230 pounds, although this figure was probably a few coconuts off. This undoubtedly led to his developing knee problems long before he had any arm wearies.

Sid was still instrumental in the Mets' revival, going 6-6 in '84 (surrendering 74 hits in 90 innings), 9-9 in '85 (2.80 ERA, 180 K's in $170^1/_3$ innings) before finally breaking out in '86 with a 16-6 record (200 K's), for an aggregate hits to innings pitched ratio of a remarkable 6.64 hits per 9 IP, plus 8.56 K's per 9 IP. He had injury-plagued seasons in '87 & '88, but still managed to win 24 games and maintain his brilliant statistics. Sid had perhaps his best all-around year in '89, when he tied Scott Garrelts (of the pennant-winning Giants) with the best winning percentage in the N.L. (.737). He pitched a career high of $219^1/_3$ innings, giving up 157 hits, to go with 198 strikeouts and a 2.83 ERA. Fernandez had an off year in '90, dropping to 9-14, but tied for 15th in the N.L. in ERA (with Chicago's Greg Maddux at 3.46), and was fourth in strikeouts with 181. The fans at Shea had taken a liking to Sid's penchant for "punchin'-em-out," and began their own version of the K-Corner, adding S's in front the letters ID to tally the number of strikeouts he had compiled in that particular game.

It was soon after, as the team started back in a losing direction that Sid's health began deteriorating. His weight problems had caused unforeseen trauma in his legs and back, which altered his pitching motion, and most students of the game know what *that* leads to: arm troubles. Sid's last great season with the Mets was in '92 when he was 10th in ERA with a 2.73 clip and 4th in strikeouts with 193, to go along with a 14-11 record. He finished up his career in '95 with the Philadelphia Phillies, but still is among the all-time leaders in victories and strike-outs as a New York Met. If there's one specific game Sid will be remembered for it's the 7th Game of the '86 Series. He bailed the Mets out of trouble, holding the Boston Red Sox at bay for 2$^{2}/_{3}$ perfect relief innings. He had been pulled from the starting rotation due to the Mets' opponent (being predominantly right-handed hitters) and their home stadium, Fenway Park, which can be murder on lefties who get a lot of fly outs. His relief stint enabled the Mets to come from behind and beat the Crimson Hose for the World Championship.

#13 Low Quality Move—A Long Day's Journey into Knight

Part of the allure and success of the '86 Mets was their diversity and how each player made use of their talent for the good of the greater whole. For Len Dykstra and Wally Backman, the centerfielder and second baseman that usually platooned vs. righties, their job was to be "table setters." They were the "pepper pots," as Phil Rizzuto would call them, responsible for getting on base, upsetting the rhythm of the opposing pitchers and providing baserunners for Keith Hernandez, Gary Carter, and Darryl Strawberry to drive in. RBI was the onus of the "meat" of the order and they came through with a total of 281 between "The Big Three." Ray Knight and Kevin Mitchell, although it was not originally intended, became the "enforcers." When it seemed the team was lacking spirit or an attempt was made to intimidate the Mets, either Knight or Mitchell or both would invariably step in and set the record straight.

Besides the aforementioned rhubarbs, both of them would come up with a clutch hit or play at an opportune moment, or just cheer their teammates on. It was Mitchell and Knight (in that order) who kept the Mets' improbable run in Game 6 of the '86 World Series going, and they scored the tying and winning runs, respectively. Two nights later, Knight hit the home run in the 7th inning that gave the Mets the lead they never surrendered in the clincher. For his 2 HR & 9 RBI, Knight was named Series M.V.P.

Knight was a free agent but fully expected to be re-signed by the Mets. It was theorized that, as had happened several times during the season, that Knight would remain at third, Howard Johnson would take over at shortstop, and Rafael Santana would step into the role of backup utility infielder. The Mets reportedly offered a 1-year deal worth $880,000, a handsome sum of money for a 34-year old third baseman who'd had 1 good season and 1 excellent post-season. Knight himself most likely would have signed, but his agent gambled on demanding another year at little less per annum ($800,000). He rolled the dice and crapped out. The Mets made no counter offer and Knight signed with the Baltimore Orioles at considerably less than either figure he had sought. Within two years, Knight retired as an active player.

Knight eventually made it to being the Cincinnati Reds' manager for a while, then got a "real promotion" up to the broadcast booth. When the Mets released him, even though Howard Johnson was waiting in the wings, they lost a lot of their character, guts, and refusal to lose. The New York Mets lost a lot of their punch, in more ways than one.

Getting rid of Mitchell seemed to be, at that moment, not a bad idea. First, the Mets had received a player from San Diego in exchange who they had coveted for quite awhile: outfielder Walter Kevin McReynolds. In fact, Cashen said at the press conference announcing the trade: "All we expect from Kevin is a 'normal' season." If McReynolds could have had consistently "normal" seasons like '87 (.276/29/95) & '88 (.288/27/99), the latter of which he "showed" in the N.L. M.V.P. voting, then Mets fans might have considered it a good deal in the long run. Unfortunately, McReynolds' "normal season" was to underachieve, spend long terms on the disabled list with foot problems, and whine and moan that he shouldn't be called upon to play centerfield. Now, ballplayers have had legitimate gripes throughout baseball history, but this is probably the first time anyone ever muttered that they had to "think about" playing centerfield for their team, and ultimately refuse it. Naturally, the "boo-birds" at Shea targeted him and, as he took refuge by withdrawing further, McReynolds became known as "The Stone Man," someone who wouldn't argue no matter how ridiculous the call. His personality became the signature of the Mets of the late '80's and early '90's.

Mitchell was the complete antithesis of McReynolds. He was brash, outspoken, aggressive, and would play any position the club asked him to. At one time or another, in his short tenure with the Mets, he played all infield and outfield spots. There's little doubt that if requested, Mitchell would have donned the catching gear, too.

Mitchell unequivocally was the most imposing player of the club, and with teammates such as Ray Knight, Len Dykstra, Wally Backman, Mookie Wilson, Keith Hernandez, and Gary Carter, there was enough "rah-rah" to fill up all the cheerleading squads in the nation. He also proved himself a good hitter (.277/12/43) in 108 games, and being only 24, much greater things were expected of him.

However, Mitchell soon began getting a reputation as being a bad influence on Dwight Gooden and Darryl Strawberry. While Mitchell was far from being perfect (especially with regard to his temper), Gooden and Strawberry ultimately must take account for their *own* actions. By ostensibly protecting "The Black

Walter Johnson" and "The Black Ted Williams," Mets' management felt it was easier to get rid of Mitchell.

Mitchell started the '87 season in his native San Diego, but was part of a multi-player deal between the Padres and the Giants, and he took his act North to the Bay Area. The trade eventually paid off for both teams within 2 years as the Padres' Mark Davis would win the N.L. Cy Young Award and Mitchell would have the season of a lifetime.

Meanwhile, Mitchell was a composite .280/22/70 in helping lead San Francisco to its first division title in 16 years and just missed upsetting the St. Louis Cardinals in the NLCS. After holding a 3-2 lead in games, the Giants were "oh-fer" the Busch, and the Cards had their third N.L. pennant in six years. The next year Mitchell contributed 19 HR & 80 RBI as the regular leftfielder, but in 1989, he literally busted out. He hit .291, slugged .635, and smacked a majors' high of 47 HR & 125 RBI. "Mitch" even made a play for the highlight reel. In Philadelphia, he was chasing a high fly ball into the corner, when as he was braking at the side fence, a door came open. Mitchell braced himself with his gloved left hand and instinctively caught the ball barehanded over his head. That play, as much as any offensive statistic, underscored his incredible M.V.P. season. This time, the Giants knocked off the Chicago Cubs in 5 games in the NLCS and clinched their first pennant in 27 years. The '89 Series will have the misfortune of being known as the "Earthquake Series." Moments before Game 3 was scheduled to start, a massive earthquake hit the Bay Area, knocking out power to the entire region. Ten days later, when it was determined that all emergency measures had been secured, the Series resumed. Oakland swept the Giants convincingly, never once relinquishing a lead. Kevin Mitchell could still hold his head high: he had hit 2 HR in the NLCS and another in the World Series, giving him a total of 50, including the regular season.

"Mitch" began experiencing weight-gain problems and although he had many other productive seasons, he couldn't come close to matching his dream season of '89. In fact, of the ten players who have won an M.V.P. Award who had at one time or another were on the Mets' roster, Mitchell is one of two that ever won the award *after* his Met tenure (the other, ironically enough, being a fellow Giant: Jeff Kent).

#14 Low Quality Move—A Hardware Shortage

Usually, when a team finds itself overabundant at a regular position, the normal course of action is to keep the better and trade the lesser. In 1989, the Mets had Kevin McReynolds and Darryl Strawberry ensconced on the outfield "corners." Directly "in the middle" the Mets were faced with a dilemma most ball clubs would have been delighted with. They had both Mookie Wilson and Len Dykstra available to play centerfield. Both were extremely capable batters and fielders, and neither was enamored with the platoon system Manager Johnson was employing. Wilson would play vs. lefties and Dykstra vs. righties. In June, after a third of a season of implementing this arrangement, Cashen made a decision: he decided to keep Wilson. Even though he was 7 years older, he was a better all-around batter, being a switch-hitter with a lifetime .281 hitter compared with Dykstra's .279. Mookie played all three outfield positions well, whereas "Nails" *only* wanted to be in centerfield (the polar opposite of "The Stone Man"). Additionally, Mookie could be moved up and down the batting order with little fuss while Dykstra would be obsessive about being in the leadoff spot.

Those factors led to Dykstra, along with relief pitcher Roger McDowell, being traded to Philadelphia for Juan Samuel. More than any other deal, this simply "tore the heart" right out of the Mets. Gone were two of the more colorful and spirited of all the Mets. In return, they obtained a second baseman they didn't need. It did, momentarily, solve their centerfield squabble, but that was made academic a month later when *Wilson was traded*, too! Mookie ended up in Toronto and helped lead them to the A.L. East title.

Meanwhile, the Mets could truly be called a "doughnut" defensive team: they had no one in the center. They tried converting Samuel, but that proved disastrous. They kept trying other infielders but did not do what they should have done in the first place: retained at least *one* of their centerfielders. The Mets finally signed one the following April, picking up Daryl Boston of the White Sox off the waiver list. Dykstra would, for 3 of the next 4 seasons, be the premier centerfielder in the N.L. In 1993, he led the league in hits and runs, was runner-up in the M.V.P. voting, and hit 4 HR in the Phillies' 6-game defeat in the World Series. Cashen, usually such a good judge of talent, outsmarted himself and temporarily left the team ¼ empty "up the middle."

#15 Combined High & Low Quality Move—B.O. Gives the Finger

Who was the top winner of the Mets' '86 World Championship pitching staff? The first reaction of most people would most likely be Dwight Gooden, who won 17 games during the regular season, but was winless in the postseason. Sid Fernandez had 16 victories, but lost Game 4 of the NLCS and was subsequently dropped from the World Series rotation and had no decisions. Ron Darling won 15 and was bailed out of a loss in Game 3 of the NLCS thanks to Len Dykstra's dramatic walk-off homer. Then Darling was victimized by Tim Teufel's 7th inning error in World Series Game 1, which resulted in the only run. He was conversely the beneficiary of his team's 9-run outburst as the Mets evened up the Series at 2-2. After the Mets' phenomenal comeback from the brink of elimination in Game 6 and a 1-day rain delay, Darling started Game 7, but surrendered 3 runs in $2^1/_3$ innings and was yanked. Roger McDowell won 14 games as both a starter and right-hand closer, but would have had to have secured 6 of the Mets' 8 postseason victories in order to even match the man who is the correct answer: Bob Ojeda.

Ojeda had been obtained from Boston in the off-season in a deal involving 8 players, with young reliever Calvin Schiraldi being the main component in the swap. Ojeda, an expert in changing speeds and pitching to spots, immediately became a Met fan favorite, especially when he used his patented "dead fish" change-up against right-handed batters. Ojeda finished with an 18-5 record, a 2.57 ERA and 148 strikeouts, establishing himself as the unofficial ace of a *terrific* (sorry, *he* was on the *other* side, by now) staff. Bob then followed that up with a 5-1 victory in the Game 2 of the NLCS. Then, in Game 6, after allowing 3 first-inning runs, he settled down and didn't allow any more runs for 6 innings, giving the Mets a chance to tie the game in the 9th and force the longest and one of the most exciting postseason contests and eventually win 7-6 in 16 innings, clinching the N.L. pennant. Winning this game meant not having to face Mike Scott in a Game 7.

Being emotionally drained, the Mets proceeded to lose the first 2 games of the World Series at home. Manager Johnson was flayed alive in the press for allowing his team an off day instead calling a practice before Game 3 at Fenway Park. Johnson had 2 reasons: 1 was that his team was physically and mentally exhausted and needed the rest. The second reason was that he had Ojeda starting, a lefty who'd had good success at Fenway Park because of his peculiar pitching style. Ojeda came through, giving up only 1 run in 7 innings as the Mets "got off the schneid." Bob also started the do-or-die 6th game on 3 days rest and allowed only 2 runs in 6 innings and left with no decision. Between the regular season and the postseason, Ojeda was 20-5 for an .800 winning percentage, and 4 quality post-season starts when the Mets absolutely needed a victory.

The next season, the entire pitching staff that had been the toast of baseball was now simply toast. Gooden missed 2 months due to drug rehab, Fernandez missed a whole month suffering tendonitis of the knee and was only 4 games over .500, Darling broke his right thumb fielding a bunt bare-handed, and newcomer David Cone was hit by a pitch and had the pinky on his pitching hand fractured. Ojeda was not immune to the strange rash of injuries; he experienced elbow chips, which required surgery and posted a mere 3-5 record. Despite collecting 92 victories, the Mets still came in 2nd, 3 games out.

By 1988, the team seemed to be back on track. Gooden won 18, Darling 17, and although Fernandez was not fully up to par (this time only 2 games over .500), Cone had a season that would surely have won an N.L. Cy Young Award (maybe even an M.V.P.) had it not occurred this year and if he'd had someone like Tom LaSorda hawking for him. Cone had an incredible 20-3 record for an amazing .874 winning percentage—among the highest single season marks of all-time. He was also second in the league in ERA (2.22) and first among anyone with 200 or more innings (sound familiar?). Cone was also runner-up to Houston's Nolan Ryan in strikeouts, 228 to 213. Implausibly, Cone wasn't even "Cy" runner-up; Danny Jackson of Cincinnati "placed" behind Orel Hershiser and his 59 consecutive scoreless innings in his last 8 starts. LaSorda, manager of the L.A. Dodgers, successfully campaigned the writers to vote for Hershiser to win the Cy Young.

Ojeda was having a decent season, although he was 3 games under .500, he had been "non-supported" a good deal of the time, as his 2.88 ERA will attest. However, Ojeda's I.Q. must have been somewhere in the single digits—liter-ally—when he went to landscape around his house using electric hedge-clippers—*one week before the playoffs*. The end result was that Ojeda sliced off the tip of his left middle finger, had to be rushed to the hospital, had an emergency grafting done, but which made him miss the NLCS, which the Mets consequently lost in seven games. Why Ojeda would choose to endanger his livelihood (and the team's fortunes) at any time, let alone right before the postseason was scheduled to start, is a question that has dumbfounded baseball fans.

His disregard for his own life resurfaced tragically five years later, as a boat being driven by him, along with Cleveland Indians' teammates Steve Olin and Tim Crews crashed into a dock in Florida during spring training. They had all been drinking heavily, the throttle was wide open, and Olin and Crews were killed. Ojeda managed to escape with minor injuries and scot-free of any criminal charges. However, his reputation as an irresponsible, reckless, loose cannon was permanently confirmed.

He was able to get one last shot at a job in the "bigs:" a tryout with the New York Yankees in '94 at the request of owner George Steinbrenner, if only to nettle the Mets. Ojeda actually made the team as a left-handed long reliever, but quickly flopped when the "boo-birds" descended upon him, constantly feeding into his "survivor's guilt."

The Mets couldn't have been so nearly successful in 1986 without Ojeda's contributions. Contrarily, his inability and unwillingness to take proper care of himself cost both him and the team dearly in the long run.

#16 Low Quality Move—Bye Bye 'Berry'

As much of a nuisance, to put it politely, Darryl Strawberry could be, few players had the offensive numbers he did in his eight years as a New York Met. He was the N.L. Rookie-of-the-Year in 1983, M.V.P. runner-up in 1988, and became the first Met to be a member of the "30-30" club. He averaged 31.5 HR & 92.1 RBI per season over his Met tenure. His emergence coincided with the Mets' revival just as his departure signaled that there were difficult times ahead.

This does not mean that Darryl was never reprimanded in the media by his manager or his teammates for his behavior or attitude. When being positioned around the outfield by coaches depending upon the scouting report of a particular batter, he often wound up drifting back to his usual spot, sometimes leaving him unable to field the ball where it was already predetermined to be most likely hit. Mets' broadcaster Tim McCarver pointed that out several times and even had the camera crew take an aerial view of what he dubbed "The Strawberry Patch." It was a very small parcel of rightfield at Shea from which Darryl rarely strayed.

Other times, he was fined for skipping practices, which Manager Johnson (whose term with the Mets was bookended by Strawberry's) never followed up with suspensions, possibly fearing repercussions, the worst of which would be Darryl's intentionally "dogging it." He did that enough without further motivation.

There were also fights with teammates, the most infamous of which was with Keith Hernandez at a team photograph shooting. Hernandez retaliated by telling members of the press that in '88, Strawberry wasn't even M.V.P. of the team, let alone the league. Whether this bit of dissension, plus Dodgers' manager Tom LaSorda's pandering cost Strawberry votes from the writers, is hard to say. The end result was that L.A.'s Kirk Gibson was selected N.L. M.V.P. and Strawberry finished second, but put on his outwardly nonchalant façade.

Strawberry exhibited this nonchalance when he was brought up on assault charges by his first wife. The pervading joke was that his wife must be right-handed because he can't hit lefties. Facing possible jail time was no joke, but soon a pattern of "enabling" began to develop, whereby Strawberry could get away with almost anything, as long as he can produce on the field. Hindsight is often 20-20, as the saying goes, but perhaps many of his future troubles could have been avoided had proper action been taken at the appropriate time. This is too frequently a "broken record" with athletes.

Strawberry, despite hitting 29 HR and driving in 77 in '89, was battling alcoholism the entire season and finally entered the Betty Ford Clinic. After extensive (and expensive) treatment, he was given a clean bill of health for 1990, which was his "walk year," the last season of his contract before he became a free agent. The Mets opted not to trade Darryl and let the dice roll. In one way, their gamble paid off because Strawberry had one of his best seasons, hitting .277, socking 37 HR and setting a new team record of 108 RBI. He helped lead the Mets to another second place finish, this time losing out to the Pittsburgh Pirates. The way the risk did not pan out was that Darryl *did* wind up "walking," signing a long-term contract with the Dodgers, determined to go home to his "native" Los Angeles a "conquering hero." After Strawberry's exodus, the Mets finished "out-of-the-money" for six straight years. The fact that they got little more than a draft choice in return hurt the team in terms of morale, productivity, and unity.

#17 Low Quality Move—The Vince Coleman 'Error'

Perhaps the strangest idea Frank Cashen ever had as Mets' general manager is that signing Vince Coleman would be a panacea for losing Darryl Strawberry. It was thought that Coleman would play the role of "table-setter," getting on base, upsetting pitchers' rhythms, and giving incumbent RBI men such as Howard Johnson, Kevin McReynolds, and Greg Jefferies chances to drive him in. After all, Coleman had set the rookie record of 110 stolen bases (while winning 1985 N.L. ROTY) and holds the mark of having a hundred or more steals in each of his first three years. He also led the N.L. in stolen bases his first six seasons, totaling 549 and looking like a sure bet to someday catch Rickey Henderson, who was on the threshold of breaking Lou Brock's lifetime record. However, the remainder of his offensive skills had begun to ebb, and he was never considered a good defensive player.

So, the Mets went ahead with Coleman as a catalyst, for better or worse. What they got was mostly worse. The Mets should have remembered his tussle with the automatic tarpaulin at St. Louis during the '85 NLCS. Coleman accidentally got his leg caught and broken, and he was forced to miss the remainder of the play-offs and the entire World Series. That should have been a harbinger of bizarre events to come.

Another omen the management should have seen was when he stopped being the league steals leader. Perhaps all that hard running and sliding had taken its toll, playing so many games on the artificial turf at Busch Stadium. In any case, Marquis Grissom of the Montreal Expos was the standard bearer with 78 and Coleman's total sank to 29.

Another peculiar incident happened in midseason when Coleman had a public argument on the field during batting practice at Shea. In front of other players and coaches, the media, fans in the stands, and manager Bud Harrelson (who, by now, had replaced Johnson), Coleman berated coach Mike Cubbage for several minutes. Harrelson's tepid response to this outrage was, "Well, he [Coleman] got four hits yesterday, so we'll see what happens." What *happens* is that modern athletes are too often "molly-coddled," and that contributes to their misbehavior at a higher level.

As if being a self-fulfilling prophecy, the following year Coleman, Dwight Gooden and Daryl Boston were all charged with sexually assaulting a woman in a hotel room at Port St. Lucie, Florida. The charges were eventually dropped due to lack of evidence (it was *her* word against theirs that sex was consensual), but it left another permanent liability in Coleman's "behavioral ledger."

Another incident involved him getting into a pushing and shoving match with manager Jeff Torborg at home plate during a game at Shea. Coleman had just been ejected for arguing a called strike and Torborg was merely trying to intervene to save Coleman from possible league disciplinary action. Instead, Coleman turned on Torborg, telling him he didn't want to be touched or told what to do. Perhaps Torborg should have just let him follow through on his tantrum, hit the umpire, and be banned from baseball.

It seemed that Coleman could be counted upon for mediocre play *on* the field and at least one disgraceful incident a year *off* it. The penultimate came on the Mets' second West Coast swing in 1993. Coleman reportedly threw a lit firecracker into a young girl's face, simply because she wanted his autograph as he was getting into his rented vehicle outside Dodger Stadium. Several other Met players were involved, including Bobby Bonilla (who's got his own upcoming negative chapter), but Coleman was the one implicated by dozens of witnesses. At first, Coleman tried to deny it, then downplay it once the tempest of publicity had spread nationwide. The girl's family wanted to press charges and sue, but a settlement was reached before anything went to court. Coleman himself gave an impassioned news conference telling of the settlement, and while he seemed genuinely chastened, never officially apologized to the victim.

This was the last straw as far as the Mets' front office was concerned. Coleman was given his unconditional release in August '93, but the Mets were obligated to "eat" the rest of his contract. What it should have taught them was think clearly and carefully *before* deciding to sign somebody, not *after* the damage has been done.

#18 Low Quality Move—"Booby Bum"

This text is teeming with adages, but one that most applies with regards to the Mets' front office mistakes is "once bitten, twice shy." By the end of 1991, when the team was in the midst of its accelerated fall from grace, someone within the organization *might* have realized the folly of blindly signing free agents. Surely, those in authority must have caught on to the secret of building a good farm system and making astute trades. However, it seems that Mr. Cashen may have just been a figurehead by now.

Apparently, the Mets' management hadn't learned its lesson from the Vince Coleman fiasco and signed Pittsburgh Pirates' third baseman/outfielder Bobby Bonilla to a whopping $29 million contract, the most lucrative in baseball history at the time. At the press conference announcing his acquisition, Bonilla reportedly commented, "I dare you all to wipe the smile off my face." *That* didn't take very long.

The honeymoon lasted exactly 1 day as Bonilla hit 2 homers, including the game winner in extra innings, Opening Night at Busch Stadium. From thereon, it was downhill as he compiled a .249 average with 19 HR & 70 RBI. The Mets were expecting more from this lineup containing Eddie Murray, Greg Jefferies, Howard Johnson, Kevin Bass, Dick Schofield Jr. and, yes, Coleman, who created havoc the relatively few times he got on base. Add to that a superlative pitching staff (on paper) of Gooden, Bret Saberhagen, Frank Viola, David Cone, and Sid Fernandez, with John Franco out of the bullpen. However, baseball is played on dirt and grass (sometimes polyturf), *not* paper. The chemistry just was never there. Believe it or not, the worst was yet to come in 1993.

In 1992, Cone had his own sexual dispute with a different woman at a different time and place. The Mets dealt him to Toronto for Ryan Thompson and Jeff Kent in time to be eligible for the '92 postseason. Viola had left a "sinking ship" through free agency (although the Mets made a generous arbitration offer). Torborg was fired at the end of May and was replaced by someone who was thought to be a strict disciplinarian: Dallas Green. Anthony Young, who'd lost his last 14 decisions the year before, continued his futility into this season as his losing streak ran to a record 27 in a row. Then came the infamous firecracker morass, involving Coleman and Bonilla whom the hostile press often referred to as "Booby Bum," a parody of his self-proclaimed nickname, "Bobby Bo." However, the comedic version was very appropriate.

The remainder of his Met tenure was just as rocky. On one occasion, Bonilla threw a temper tantrum when the third base coach held up a runner from third base after he had hit a short fly ball with less than two outs and the Mets trailing by five runs. Bonilla childishly felt that coach Cubbage had deliberately denied him an RBI and cost him an at-bat. History had repeated itself when the manager would not back the same coach who had been the target of two different selfish players' invective.

It was a microcosm of the utterly disastrous season (which, of course, included the firecracker incident) and the Mets compiled a 59-103 record, their worst since 1965 and the first rock bottom finish in a decade. They needed rebuilding once again.

Murray, despite having back-to-back 100 RBI seasons, got fed up with the situation and signed with Cleveland. HoJo retired when he felt he couldn't perform the way he used to and was offered a minor-league coaching job. Saberhagen was enjoying an excellent 14-4 record when the strike struck on August 11, 1994, wiping out the remainder of the regular season and the postseason. However, both Saberhagen and Fernandez developed severe arm troubles and had to prematurely retire.

As for Bonilla, he was traded to Baltimore for highly touted prospect Alex Ochoa in 1995, with several other players involved. Of course, while seeking a new contract, Bonilla knuckled down and had a .287/28/116 season for the O's, helping lead them as far as the ALCS. As usual, he eventually wore out his welcome and ultimately wound up in 1999 with, of all teams, the Mets. Perhaps new general manager Steve Phillips was having a pipe dream when he thought he was getting back a more "competitive, driven" Bonilla. Though he contributed next to nothing as a pinch hitter, except for his "ubiquitous" smile, he was still included on the postseason roster.

In the 6th Game of the NLCS, Bonilla showed his true "competitiveness" and "drive" by playing cards with Rickey Henderson in the Atlanta visiting clubhouse. The Mets lost to the Braves, who won their 3rd N.L. pennant in 5 years. Although they retained Henderson until the middle of the next season, the Mets were finally smart enough to release "Booby Bum" for good.

#16 High Quality Move—The Return of Bobby V.

The Mets have long had a penchant, as previously noted, to obtain players past their prime. Such was the case of Bobby Valentine. He had once been a top prospect in the Dodgers organization, but an unfortunate collision with an outfield wall resulted in a broken leg. This set his career back irreparably and made him available on the trading block. Although he tried his best, he was clearly not the same player as before the accident, and since the Mets were in a declining phase in the late '70's, they simply couldn't afford "carrying" him.

Valentine took the rejection in stride and went about the process of succeeding in the majors by managing in the minors. He finally made it back to the bigs in 1984 as one of Davy Johnson's coaches. Johnson gives credit to Valentine by his aggressiveness, showing baserunners to take chances instead of being complacent. That year, the Mets went from 68-94 to 90-72, and from last place to second. Within a month of the start of the '85 season, Valentine interviewed for the position of managing the Texas Rangers and was offered the job. He really wanted to stay with this rapidly rising Mets' squad instead of taking over the downtrodden Rangers, but opportunities such as this don't come around very often. With Johnson's blessing, Bobby took over the helm in Arlington.

After being there nearly a decade, he then had the rare alternative to return to New York and help the Mets rebound to their past glory. In his first full season, 1997, the Mets posted an 88-74 record, the most victories they'd had in 7 years. The following year they brought home the identical record, with one sad footnote that they lost their last 5 games, when one win would have secured the "Wild Card" berth. Though this was disappointing, these two highly successful campaigns rejuvenated the hopes of Mets' fans. As was the case 13 years before, the third time proved to be the charm, as the Mets finished in a tie with the Cincinnati Reds at 96-66, and Al Leiter threw a two-hit shutout at Cinergy Field in the Wild Card Playoff. In the NLDS, the Mets defeated the Arizona Diamondbacks in four games, swamping Cy Young Award winner Randy Johnson in the opener and clinching on a dramatic walk-off homer by backup catcher Todd Pratt.

From there, they went on to the NLCS, facing their newest heated rivals, the Atlanta Braves. The Mets lost the first three games and could easily have folded their tents. However, Bobby Valentine had helped toughen and mold his team to a more durable tenacious determined bunch. They avoided a sweep, then won a dramatic seesaw 13-inning affair, culminating in Robin Ventura's famous "grand slam single." The Braves did the Mets a similar turn in Game 6, pushing across the winning run when Andruw Jones extracted a bases-loaded walk from Kenny Rogers. The fact that the Mets had completely worn down the Braves was evident when the Yankees swept Atlanta in the World Series. More great things were expected of Valentine's crew in the future.

The Y2K proved to be the future for the Mets. They had to "settle" for the Wild Card again, since the Braves managed one more victory than they did (95 to 94). However, as Bobby had on more than one occasion pointed out regarding the current playoff system, it was most important just to make it to the "Final Four." His assertion was confirmed when the Mets knocked off the San Francisco Giants, the team with the best record during the regular season, and the Braves were similarly upended by the St. Louis Cardinals. The Mets dominated the NLCS, winning in five games, with a beanball war perpetrated by the frustrated Cards providing the only real drama. It did damage the Mets chances in the World Series as shortstop Mike Bordick had his thumb fractured and went hitless vs. (guess who) the Yankees. The real key to the Mets losing the first Subway Series in 44 years may have been letdowns in the lidlifter on the parts of two gentlemen whose names end in "ez:" Timo Perez and Armando Benitez.

Perez was on first base when Todd Zeile (whose moniker begins with Ze; an interesting juxtaposition) hit a deep drive to leftfield that bounced off the top of the fence at Yankee Stadium. Instead of running hard the entire way, Perez chose to admire Zeile's majestic power and didn't "turn on the jets" until it was too late. His getting thrown out at the plate ended a potential big inning and left the Mets precariously holding a one-run lead. Still, their closer Benitez, who had been so reliable all year since taking over when John Franco was temporarily sidelined, should have been able to hold the vanguard. Then, Yankees' rightfielder Paul O'Neill worked a 12-pitch walk and the rest was history. The Yanks rallied to pull out Game 1 in 12 innings, Roger Clemens intimidated the entire Met team by throwing a broken bat at Mike Piazza, and when action returned to Shea Stadium, the Mets lost two out of three. Their dream season was suddenly ended.

As despondent as the Mets and their fans were, everything was horrifically put into perspective 10½ months later on September 11, 2001. The Mets were still very much in the playoff hunt, but all that was put on hold as a city and a nation sought to recover. Bobby Valentine did as much hands-on work helping the relief effort as anybody, but it may have taken its toll on his managerial skills. His team finished six games out of first place after making an inspired run to close within 1½ of tying. The next season, the Mets literally bottomed out, finishing in the cellar for the first time since their most shameful season of 1993, and were 11 games under .500.

At first, it seemed Valentine would be spared the axe, especially since the club's fortunes had improved every season of his tenure. Despite frequent disagreements with GM Steve Phillips, Valentine's position appeared to be secure, considering all his well-documented volunteer efforts. However, Mets' high brass must have followed Branch Rickey's aforementioned credo of "a year too early instead of a year too late" and dismissed Bobby two days after the end of the 2002 regular season.

Thus ended one of the most flamboyant eras in team history. Managing in an environment where every move is publicly calculated and second-guessed, Valentine did his best to revitalize a dormant organization. He would even provide comic relief when necessary, such as the time when he came back into the dugout after being ejected sporting a fake moustache and dark glasses. The league fined him, but his team responded and subsequently went on a winning streak.

As Casey Stengel was famous for saying, "I couldn't have done it (won) without my players." That condition is necessary for all managers and coaches. Bobby Valentine need not further prove his winning ways, on *and* off the field.

#17 High Quality Move—Throwback to Mex (OLĔ)

While the adage goes that a team must be strong up the middle (pitcher, catcher, second baseman, shortstop, and centerfielder) in order to be successful, the four corners must be solid as well. By 1997, it had been a decade since the Mets had a full-time reliable first baseman and that had led directly to their decline. Shortly before Xmas the previous year, they would get a present from the Toronto Blue Jays which would pay huge dividends for the ensuing three seasons: John Olerud.

Olerud had never played a game in the minors, having come straight from the University of Washington to the Blue Jays in 1989. He didn't get to see action in the ALCS that year but he became Toronto's starting first sacker by the middle of the following season. He had "Norm Cash"-like success his first seven years: in 1993, he hit over .300 the only time in his years with Toronto, but won the batting title, finishing at .363. In fact, the Blue Jays pulled off something that's been done only once in the history of Major League Baseball: the top three batters in terms of average came from the same team. Paul Molitor was runner-up at .332 and Roberto Alomar (we'll get to him later) followed at .326. Olerud was a key member of the Blue Jays' back-to-back World Championships and showed rare class by not publicly sulking when he was platooned due to the lack of a designated hitter being used in the National League home games.

Over the next three seasons, Olerud "slumped" to a .287 average, which was still better than many others. The Blue Jays were in a rebuilding/salary-dumping mode when they traded Olerud to the Mets even-up for pitcher Robert Person. The acquisition of such an excellent fielding first baseman instantly improved the other three Mets infielders (the four regulars had an aggregate total of 42 errors) and gave them a steady bat as well (.294/22/102 with a team high of 85 walks). This was just a prelude.

In 1998, while most of the baseball world was focused on Mark McGwire's and Sammy Sosa's pursuit of Roger Maris' single season home run record, Olerud quietly put together one of the best all-around years in Mets' history. He shattered Cleon Jones' team record .340 batting average by 13 percentage points and for all intents and purposes actually won the N.L. batting title. Larry Walker of the Colorado Rockies hit .363, but had a ridiculous "split" in his home-and-away average: a mile-high aided .418 compared to .302 on the road.

John also drew 95 bases-on-balls, scored 91 runs, compiled 36 doubles and 22 home runs as part of his 197 hits. In the field, Olerud was phenomenal: he committed only 5 errors in 1,379 chances for a league leading .996 fielding percentage. Had the Mets not completely collapsed the last week of the season and the Yankees not had a record-smashing year of their own, Olerud would have gotten more notoriety.

Perhaps it was this climate of too much criticism and not enough acclaim that made Olerud want to seek the greener pastures of his native Pacific Northwest. One New York writer even sunk so low as to make fun of John's having to wear a helmet in the field to protect his skull due to an aneurysm. Olerud's response was to let his bat and mitt do the talking for him, as he was never the most verbose person to begin with.

He had another steady season in 1999, hitting .298 with 19 homers and 96 RBI, while setting a team record of 125 walks. This time, Olerud did get a lot more positive exposure, which any player yearns for in a "walk" year. The Mets tied for the Wild Card, won the playoff vs. the Reds, beat the Diamondbacks in the NLDS, and gave the Braves everything they could handle and then some in the NLCS. Despite all these thrills, Olerud was determined to go home to Washington, played out his option (while turning down the Mets' arbitration offer) and signed with the Seattle Mariners. Although the Mets won the pennant the next year, Olerud's departure left a void they have yet to fill.

Olerud continued being productive, playing an important role in the Mariners' achievements in 2000 and 2001, and would appear to have many good seasons left in him. His time with the Mets could be compared to one of those "westerns" where a quiet sheriff "moseys" into town, cleans up the place of riff-raff, and idles out without much fanfare. Only those who were paying attention know the great and unheralded job he did.

#18 High Quality Move—The Pizza Man Delivers

For the all the times the New York Mets made bad trades and other transactions (and for all the times the front office was "raked over the coals" because of them), when the Mets pull off a deal that nets huge success, accolades must be paid. Such a deal occurred May 22, 1998 when they acquired superstar catcher Mike Piazza from the Florida Marlins. Piazza was in the midst of his sixth season and had just been traded a week before from the Los Angeles Dodgers.

Several years earlier, no one could have imagined this happening. The Dodgers had been owned by the O'Malley family, which usually held onto their own prospects longer than anyone. Their patience was rewarded as Piazza was 1993 N.L. Rookie of the Year, a 5-time All-Star with a .334 lifetime BA, who'd averaged 34 homers and 107 RBI despite missing a significant amount of games due to labor disputes. Additionally, Mike was the godson of Dodgers' manager Tom LaSorda. Now the Dodgers were under new ownership and LaSorda had been replaced. Piazza was seeking a long-term contract, as most players would, not only for security but also for stability. What he got instead was an unceremonious heave-ho to the team that had just won the World Series but whose owner, Wayne Huizenga, was dumping high salaries. A week later, Piazza would join the list of exiles, but the Mets would be the beneficiaries.

Ironically, a baker's dozen years before, it was the acquisition of a productive catcher that gave the Mets impetus to improve: Gary Carter. In many ways, each backstop's term with the club was similar. They both came over as the Mets were in an upswing and were seen as the "missing piece to the puzzle." Each had their team in the World Series within their first two full years. However, both suffered steady declines in their respective offensive output, mostly due to the rigors their position.

When the Mets obtained Piazza, he was still three months shy of his 30th birthday, so they could trust him to carry the team as few players ever had. For the remainder of the 1998 season, Piazza hit .348 (.329 overall) and socking 23 of his 32 homers wearing the orange-and-blue. Mike was also one of the few Mets who didn't fold the final week, batting .368 and driving in 3 of his 111 RBI. Unfortunately, except for John Olerud and Edgardo Alfonzo, no one else hit above .200 and the pitching collapsed worse. It was similar to the way the Mets had finished in 1985, just missing out on the post-season, but left with a tremendous amount of hope and confidence for the following year.

Piazza and company didn't disappoint. Mike became the second player in Met history to top 40 homers, while breaking the team record in RBI with 124. As previously mentioned (but why not mention it again considering the team's success-to-failure ratio), the Mets tied Cincinnati for the Wild Card and won the playoff game for the right to face the Arizona Diamondbacks in the NLDS. They carried the energy into an upset victory in 4 games, and then extended the Atlanta Braves to six knockdown drag 'em out contests in which the Mets had a chance to tie or win in all their final at bats.

As Carter had done in 1986, Piazza led the Mets to the pennant in 2000 with another steady season: .324/38/113 with 90 runs scored. Almost as impressive was his catching 124 games and committing only 3 errors. However, he was again snubbed by the Baseball Writers who vote for the MVP Award, as he lost out to Jeff Kent of the San Francisco Giants. This further fortified the notion that there is both an anti-New York sentiment and a prejudice against players with a "squeaky-clean" image, which also befell Gary Carter on numerous occasions. In any case, Piazza continued his great hitting through the two playoff rounds, and then slammed 2 homers and drove in 4 vs. the Yankees in the face of a 5-game defeat and Roger Clemens' "psych job."

As difficult as it is for teams to repeat, the Mets faced greater challenges in the coming year. The regulars, such as Todd Zeile, Robin Ventura, Jay Payton, as well as Piazza and Alfonzo slumped and set off a team-wide decline. Despite his reduced output, a 33-year old catcher who could put up numbers like Piazza did (.300/36/94) anywhere else would have been lauded instead of criticized. However, this type of season was at the very least becoming expected from Piazza, and he had his own excellence to try to best.

2002 saw Piazza still produce (.280/33/98) but his defensive skills were eroding (he was averaging 1 stolen base allowed per game caught—not exactly an impressive ratio) and pressure was being put on him by the media to move to first base. It's doubtful that any such position change could have prevented the Mets plummet into last place, just 2 years after they sat atop the National League. Piazza was branded with goat horns, as was Alfonzo, while other "brilliant acquisitions" such as Mo Vaughn, Roberto Alomar, and Jeromy Burnitz were absolutely pitiful but escaped wholesale vilification.

What became of Mike Piazza in 2003 is too sad to include in this tribute to him and the club(s) he has toiled for. If he had retired before this disastrous season, his totals would have looked something like this: A lifetime batting average of .321 derived from 1,641 career hits in 5,115 at bats with 347 homers and 1,073 RBI. These are all Hall-of-Fame caliber numbers, combined with his playing in the top two media markets (except for one week) of Los Angeles and New York.

This past season is not even worth mentioning; needless to say Mike and many of his teammates suffered tremendous letdowns and greatly underachieved. Hopefully, Mike can ultimately move to first base on a permanent basis so his offensive statistics can bounce back and he can be relieved of the burdens of catching. Ironically, Piazza was voted in a poll of fans as the catcher on the All-Time Mets Team. Now, in order to salvage his career, he may be forced to do the one thing he didn't want to do as a professional ballplayer: relinquish his "tools of ignorance."

Conclusion

I know in the beginning of this text I said that 21 transactions in either direction would be addressed. In fact, the title chosen was "Double Blackjack," which was supposed to be significant in both the quantity of years of the Mets' existence and their best and worst deals. As a writer, I chose to take poetic license and limit the amount to 18, "Double Chai" if you will. This is not a reference to tea; this is the Hebrew number Chai, which is the combination of ten and eight. It can also mean the word "life."

Since the lifetime of the Mets has almost paralleled mine, I decided to cut short the story and just summarize from here. Surely, the low quality moves have far outweighed the high quality moves since the Mets were able to obtain the services of Mike Piazza. He was the focal point of their being able to attain their incredible success the last years of the 20th Century. However, both his teammates and the front office have let him down ever since.

Signing Roberto Alomar was an exceptionally bad choice; worse yet was picking up his option and letting Edgardo Alfonzo go as a free agent. Alfonzo had been an organization man for many years, switching back and forth to different positions when requested and producing magnificently, both in the field and at bat. In other words, one could say the Mets opted for the "spitter instead of the hitter."

Another "splendid" maneuver was trading Kevin Appier, who'd actually been their most effective pitcher in 2001, to the Angels even up for Mo Vaughn. The best that Vaughn could do was add his name to the list on the answer to a trivia question: how many players who at one time in their careers played for the Mets won the MVP Award? The correct response is ten. However, Vaughn did not live up to his ballyhoo and had to be put on permanent disability this season due to a knee injury. This episode is a microcosm of what has happened with the Mets the last couple of seasons.

If I live to be 84, that means the Mets should play another 42 seasons. The last 42 have been filled with heartache and rapture, agitation and excitement, ups and downs, highs and lows. One fixture they'll be without is their Hall-of-Fame broadcaster Bob Murphy, who just retired and has done his last "happy recap." Hopefully, there will be many more "happy recaps" for Met fans, including a new stadium.

Information Sources

The Baseball Encyclopedia; Macmillian Publishing Co., 1979 edition.

Baseball Weekly; USA Today Publications (Gannett Co.); Volume XIII Number 28 (September 30-October 6, 1998); Volume X Number 28 (October 4–October 10, 2000); Volume XI Number 29 (October 10–October 16, 2001).

Bats: The Man Behind the Miracle, Davy Johnson and Peter Golenbock; Bantam Books, May 1987 edition.

Major League Baseball 1974; Simon & Schuster Inc., April 1974 edition.

Mets Magazine; Professional Sports Publications; Issue 5, 2002.

New York Mets 1986 Yearbook: 25th Anniversary Issue; Doubleday Sports Inc.

Sports Weekly; USA Today Publications (Gannett Co.); Volume I Number 5 (October 2–October 8, 2002).

Who's Who in Baseball; Who's Who in Baseball Magazine Co. Inc.; 1977, 1984, 1991, 1998 editions.

The World Almanac and Book of Facts; Newspaper Enterprise Association Inc.; 1974 edition.

The World Almanac and Book of Facts; PRIMEDIA Reference Inc.; 2000 edition.

The Year the Mets Lost Last Place; Paul Zimmerman and Dick Schaap; World Publishing Co.; 1969 edition.

Why Anyone Should Buy This Book

This team was literally born out of the ashes of abandonment by the Dodgers and the Giants. "Double Blackjack" tells of the origins of the New York Mets as a franchise, and traces their very modest and shaping first seven seasons, before they "tilted at windmills" in their famous Miracle Championship of 1969.

If you love to read stories (whether true or fictitious) about sports (whether about huge success stories like the New York Yankees or prodigious frustrations such as the St. Louis Browns), then this book is for you.

It follows the roller coaster ride that has been and still is the Mets' history. It focuses on some of the most dramatic characters (either respectable or despicable) that have made up the personality of the Mets' organization, which at times was an oxymoron. "Double Blackjack" also gives credit and credence to their loyal fans, who have endured so much anguish.

About the Author

Larry Liebenthal is currently employed as a Telecommunications Technical Associate/Field Technician for what used to be known as New York Telephone. He has worked there for 15 years and is nearly finished with "The Next Step Program" to earn an A.A.S. in telecommunications. He has also done freelance writing, including this book.

Mr. Liebenthal lives in Cedarhurst, New York, with his wife Roslyn, their daughter Ellen, and their cat Blackjack, who was part of the inspiration for this project.

0-595-31276-4